Los Altos: Portrait Of A Community

A Century of Photos

PREFACE

"Los Altos: Loveliest Place on the Peninsula"

Los Altos is 33 miles (by double track Southern Pacific cutoff)[1] south of San Francisco on a plateau 225 feet high adjoining the Santa Cruz Mountains. It is three miles from Stanford University, one mile from the new Santa Clara College[2], 14 miles from San Jose, all reached by double track steam railway[3] and by electric railway[4] to be finished January 1, 1910.

CROWN OF THE PENINSULA

The area bears the surname of the "Crown of the Peninsula." Whether or not it is the most beautiful townsite in California is left confidently for the reader to decide after viewing it. Immediately back rises the dark wooded walls of the Santa Cruz Mountains with lower slopes in springtime a vivid green, walls broken with picturesque canyons, home of a dashing stream, walls with forests of oak mountain laurel and giant redwoods affording in a few minutes' walk or carriage ride all the attractions of a parklike wilderness, delightful picnic and camping places.

Between the mountains and the town flows a never-failing mountain trout stream, Yeguas Creek[5]. Its banks are lined with oaks, wild cherries, buckeyes, mountain laurel and where not too swift, bordered with water cress.

But the title, Crown of the Peninsula, comes from the outlook valleyward. Los Altos, according to a railroad survey, is the first high point on its Peninsula lines–more than 150 feet higher than Palo Alto and more than 100 feet higher than San Jose.

The foothill climate of the Santa Clara Valley is famous . . . at least one government expert has pronounced the climate of the Los Altos section where the Peninsula flares into the valley as ideal and unequaled anywhere; here the mountain airs, the bay breezes and the breath of the valley mingle, the harsher characteristics of each being neutralized . . . with a Los Altos trademark . . . more days of sunshine than any other Peninsula town.

Excerpts from a 1909 Altos Land Company brochure designed to lure prospective settlers to the new community.

Footnotes: (1) Became Foothill Expressway by 1964. (2) Santa Clara University purchased 700 acres in 1904 to build a new college, but lost momentum because of the 1906 earthquake. The land is now Los Altos Country Club. (3) Discontinued in 1964. (4) Discontinued in 1933. (5) Now called Adobe Creek.

ACKNOWLEDGMENTS

In late 1991, Penny Lave, City Council member and community volunteer extraordinaire, convened a group of citizens to begin planning a celebration to mark the 40th anniversary of the incorporation of the city of Los Altos. The origina! Celebration Committee, in addition to Penny Lave, included Dick Henning, Jean Newton, Sheila Faillace, Troy Underwood, Pinky Whelan, Judy Hannemann, Connie Mraz, Joe Leal, Larry Madsen, Conrad Heintzelman, Patricia Williams, Paul Nyberg, Ginny Lear, Sue Heesaker, Jan Meyer, Marion Grimm, Bob Rayl, Jane Reed, Jo Zschau, Ed Barnes, Judith Burrill, Joanne Byrne, Anne Chappell, Ami Mills, Doyne Mraz, Carol Scharz, Louise Spangler and Nettie Tays Campbell.

As one expression of the "birthday year," the group voted to publish a hard-cover pictorial history book that would become a permanent record of the communities of Los Altos and Los Altos Hills. However, such an undertaking had two major needs: someone to get it done, and someone to fund it. Both problems were resolved quickly.

Los Altan Paul Nyberg, owner and president of Select Communications, Inc., a magazine publishing firm in Los Altos, volunteered to serve as editor and overall project coordinator. He set up a volunteer book committee of chapter authors to write an introductory essay for each chapter and to gather a "century of photos."

The second problem, a funding resource, was solved when *Los Altos Tomorrow*, the new community foundation founded by Roy Lave, Jim Reynolds and others, volunteered to underwrite the project and handle the marketing of the book as a fund-raising project.

With the book now completed, special thanks is expressed on behalf of the Birthday Committee to the authors of individual chapters whose names appear with each chapter, and to many photographers who volunteered their time and efforts.

This book would not have been possible without the dedicated support of Los Altos History House personnel, particularly Marion Grimm and Jo Zschau. Appreciation is expressed to Mary van Tamelen who gave unselfish hours to proofread the manuscript. Additional thanks is due to long term residents Anna Knapp Fitz, Marjorie Kellogg-Van Rheeden and Edgar McDowell for adding invaluable historical perspective to the project.

A final thanks to the hundreds of citizens listed at the back of the book who helped sponsor the publication by advance purchase of copies.

Dick Henning
Book Committee Chairman

DEDICATION

This book is dedicated to the
community volunteers . . .
the many men and women
whose vision and unselfish efforts
for nearly 100 years have made
Los Altos and Los Altos Hills
a special place.

Revised Edition 2000

ACKNOWLEDGEMENTS

We express special appreciation to those who made this Revised Edition 2000 possible. Thanks to Marion Grimm, whose careful reviews of proofs, corrections of dates and upgrades of information not only fixed minor errors in the original edition, but provided sound advice for new material. Emily Thurber and Francis La Poll provided helpful proofing for corrections to the first edition. Bruce Barton wrote the final chapter of this revised edition: "The Last Decade." Finally, Firooz Ghaffari added his exceptional graphics skills in reformating the pages of the previous edition and created the photo scans and design to the new pages that make this Revised Edition 2000 truly a book for the new millennium.

—Paul D. Nyberg, Editor

Where community exists
it confers upon its members identity,
a sense of belonging, a measure of security.
Individuals acquire a sense of self
partly from their continuous
relationship to others
and from the culture of their native place.

—*John Gardner*
Building Community

An endowment fund established to build a stronger community and enhance the quality of life in Los Altos and Los Altos Hills through support of philanthropic activities.

Board Members and Founders of
LOS ALTOS COMMUNITY FOUNDATION, 1999

John W. Gardner
Honorary Founder

Margaret Abe
Lois & Bob Adams
Dan Alexander
Marge & Roger Anderson
Barbara & Dushan Angius
Mona & Bob Armistead
Jan & Dennis Austin
Mickie & Wesley Ayres
Therese & Richard Baer
Lorna & Al Bagley
Shirley & Joe Bailey
Ed Barnes
Gloria & Gene Bauer
Terry & Gerry Baugus
Pat & John Blackie
Penny & Roger Brunello
Marge & Mike Bruno
Ann & Bill Bryson
Joelle & Roger Burnell
Jean & Art Carmichael
Kris & Harold Casto
Rosemary & Peter Caswell
Jeannette & Bob Chamberlain
Coeta Chambers
Betty & George Cilker
Jo & Kim Clark
Betty & Wilbur Clarke
Deborah Meredith & Curtis Cole
Claudia & Bill Coleman
Mary Linda Cook
Dee & Jim Cunningham
Elayne & Philip Dauber
Stevie & John Day
Mary & Joe Dooling
Faith & Dick Duhring
Marlene & Duane Dunwoodie
Shari & Edward Emling
Sylvia & Roger Eng
Virginia & Guy Farthing
Karen & Randy Fowler
Pat & Chet Frankenfield
Phyllis & Hank Gauthier
Dianne Gershuny
Nan & Chuck Geschke
Giti & Firooz Ghaffari
Nancy & Rick Glaze
Hon Mai & Joe Goodman
Lee & Martin Gorfinkel
Marion & Bob Grimm
Marlene & Wayne Grove
Barbara & Roy Gustafson
Judy Hannemann
Janet & Sam Harding
Leon W. Harman
Valerie & Jack Hatton
Laphalene & Ed Hawkins
Harriet & Dave Heebink
Janice & Jack Heidmiller
Helen Helson
Fran & Bill Helson
Paulette & Dick Henning
Dorothea C. Hoefler
Doni & Sid Hubbard
Carolee & Steve Hunton
Bobbie & Jack Huston
Grace & Jim Johnston
Mary Jane Johnston
Betty & Bob Joss
Mady & Mel Kahn
Rory & Dan Kaplan
Ken Kaye
Marjo & Clay Klein
Trenna & J. David Knudson
Ruth & Keith Koehler
Carol & Ralph Kuiper
Myla & Francis La Poll
Sue & Peter LaTourrette
Betty & Jerry Latta
Penny & Roy Lave
Ginny & King Lear
Louise & Bob Lee
Ann & George Limbach
Mary Cunneen- & Chip Lion
Cindy & Dave Luedtke
Ruth & Bob Lundquist
Ingrid & Tom MacDonald
Sally & John Mandle
Mary & John Mason
Edgar McDowell
Jean & Carew McFall
Nancy & Ben McGann
Lindy & Allan McLeod
Joanna & Dave Medin
Mimi & Roger Menard
Pat & Eric Millar
Becky & Jim Morgan
Jackie & John Moss
Jean Newton
Ofelia & Alex Ng
Lois & Clyde Noel
Liz & Paul Nyberg
Joanne & Fred O'Such
Louise & Stephen Pahl
Ruth Powell
Mary Prochnow
Jane & John Reed
Pat and Bob Reed
Vicki & Dave Reeder
Sandy & Joe Renati
Jim Reynolds
Richard F. Reynolds
Anne & Duane Roberts
Virginia Roberts
Kristine & Denis Salmon
Genevieve Saunders
Charlene & Walter Scholey
Pat & Steve Schott
Lee Shahinian
Marie & Walter Singer
Gerry & Goody Steinberg
Suzie & Ry Smith
Louise & Denny Spangler
Anne Leung- & Larry Stevens
Ginny & Richard Strock
Linda & John Swan
Alan Swanson
Marilyn & Lorrin Tarlton
Emily & Jim Thurber
Kay & Jon Tompkins
Nancy & Al Traficanti
Mary & Gene vanTamelen
Barbara & Ralph Vetterlein
Anne & Jim Wall
Sisi Weaver
Patti Williams / Eric Dahl
Judie & Peter Wolken
Bobbie & Dennis Young
Jo & Ed Zschau

Bank of Los Altos
Casto Roofing
Kiwanis Club of Los Altos
Los Altos Village Association
Rotary Club of Los Altos

LOS ALTOS COMMUNITY FOUNDATION has proudly sponsored this book on the history of our communities. All profits from the sale of books go the foundation and to the Los Altos History House Museum. Copies available for $25 plus local sales tax. Order from Los Altos History House Museum, 51 South San Antonio Road, Los Altos CA 94022.

CONTENTS

1937

The downtown triangle was already well defined by 1937, though still spotted with orchards. The configuration of the downtown streets—Main, State, Edith and the cross streets—is unchanged. Likewise the gentle curves of University, Orange, Palm and Burke have been maintained even though housing has replaced the open spaces.

1990

One landmark, the San Antonio School at Hillview and San Antonio Road, has disappeared and has been replaced by office buildings. Only a handful of the millions of apricot, prune and walnut trees remain in an occasional front or back yard of the thousands of homes that replaced them. Photos courtesy of Pacific Aerial Surveys, Oakland.

1

Early Roots

BY MARION GRIMM

Primitive Indians were the first inhabitants of the Los Altos area. Now called Ohlone, a Miwuk word meaning "people of the west," these peaceful natives lived an idyllic life, in harmony with nature, for at least 10,000 years before the arrival of Europeans.

The earliest expeditions into Northern California took place between 1542 and 1769. In the late 1700s California became a province of Spain and colonization began with the development of a chain of missions from San Diego to San Francisco by Father Junipero Serra. The people of the missions tried to "civilize" the Ohlones but only succeeded in enslaving them and eventually eradicating most of them.

Adobe Creek 1900. Formerly called Yeguas Creek, the stream was once a never failing water source, coming down clear and cold from the ranges above Los Altos in a succession of babbling falls and quiet pools. Yes, trout abounded. History House Museum photo.

The Spanish had issued some land grants to the Church, but when Mexico gained its independence from Spain and claimed California, the Secularization Act of 1833 stripped the Church of its great land holdings. In the early 19th century the Mexican government issued many land grants rewarding people for political reasons, military service, friendship or other favors.

Two of these land grants covered acreage that surrounds what is now Los Altos and most of Los Altos Hills. One was Rancho la Purissima Concepcion and the other Rancho San Antonio. Gradually these two large holdings were divided into 40 to 100 acre parcels and much of the land was changed from grazing land to wheat and hayfields and vineyards. The threshed grain and the wine from the vineyards were shipped from landings built on the nearby bay.

The present townsite of Los Altos was owned at one time by Mrs. Sarah Winchester, widow of the famous Winchester rifle inventor. In 1906, it was purchased by the Peninsula Interurban Railway and later by the Southern Pacific Railroad Company. The Altos Land Company, formed by Paul Shoup and others, acquired the land from the railroad and started the sale of lots for a town called *Banks and Braes*, a stop on the proposed railroad. Shortly thereafter, the name of the small settlement was changed to *Los Altos*, which means, "The Heights." □

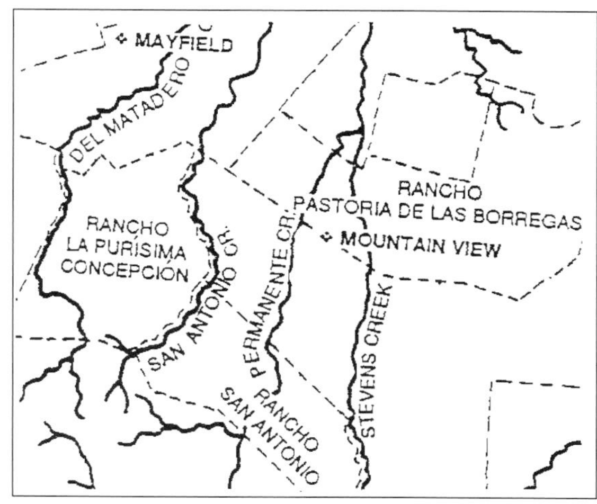

Above left: The Ohlones lived a peaceful life, usually in villages along streams or near the Bay. They had many sources of food, plenty of water, and because of the mild climate had little need for clothes or shelter, though they were known to daub their bodies with mud and build small reed huts for protection from the bright sun. Drawing from the Florence Fava Collection, courtesy of Redwood Grove Nature Preserve.

Above right: The Mexican government granted two large ranches–in 1839, Rancho San Antonio to Don Juan Prado Mesa as reward for military service, and a year later two Indians, Jose Gregorio and Jose Ramon, were granted 5,000 acres, which became Rancho La Purissima Concepcion when purchased by Dona Juana Briones De Miranda in 1850. Map from 1991 Los Altos Walking Tour Brochure .

Left: The Winchester/Merriman house at 762 Edgewood Lane is thought to be the oldest home in Los Altos, part of it possibly was built in the 1840s. At the turn of the century it housed the Chandler School for Girls. Now a private residence, it is designated a local historic landmark. History House Museum photo.

Below: Wall and patio of the Dona Juana Briones de Miranda's 1850 home still stands in 1992 as part of a later structure on Old Trace Road. History House Museum photo from the Florence Fava Collection.

1

Early Roots

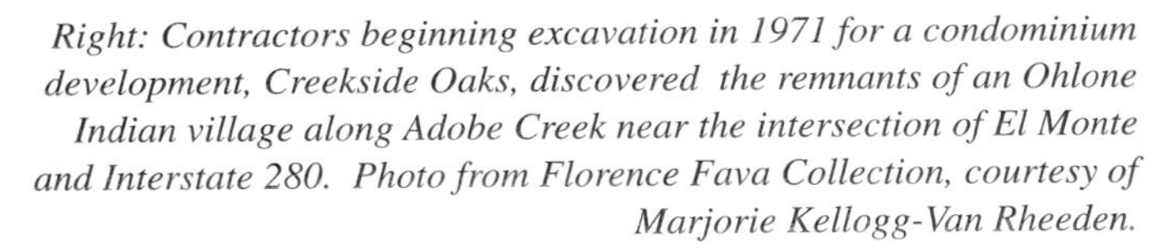

Right: Contractors beginning excavation in 1971 for a condominium development, Creekside Oaks, discovered the remnants of an Ohlone Indian village along Adobe Creek near the intersection of El Monte and Interstate 280. Photo from Florence Fava Collection, courtesy of Marjorie Kellogg-Van Rheeden.

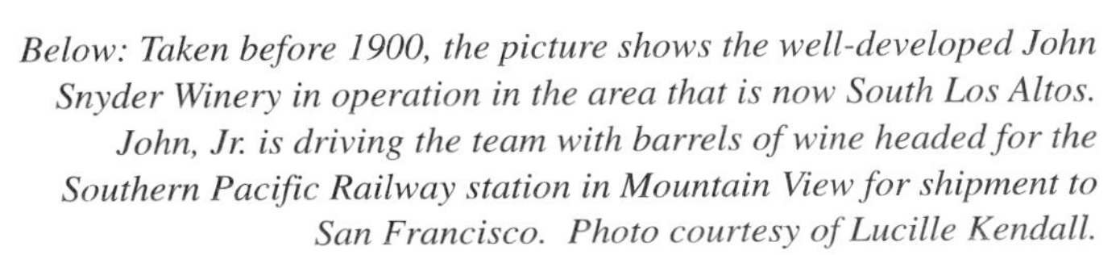

Below: Taken before 1900, the picture shows the well-developed John Snyder Winery in operation in the area that is now South Los Altos. John, Jr. is driving the team with barrels of wine headed for the Southern Pacific Railway station in Mountain View for shipment to San Francisco. Photo courtesy of Lucille Kendall.

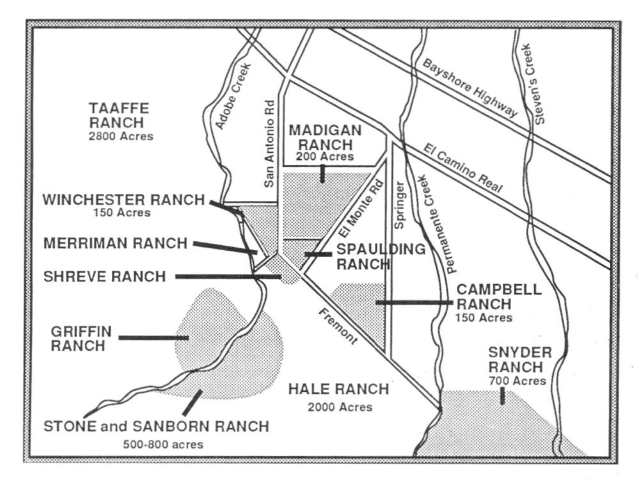

Left: Large ranches dominated the landscape in the late 19th century as shown in diagram. Fruit became the main crop on these lands as the ranches were divided into smaller and smaller acreages. In 1907 the Altos Land Company subdivided what is now the downtown area into both commercial and residential lots. History House Museum photo.

Below right: Home of Shelby Hood Kifer, brother-in-law of John Snyder, both of whom had large landholdings in the Los Altos area in the 1860s and 1870s. John Snyder grew wheat and other grain without irrigation. He also had vineyards and produced wine until disease wiped out the vines. History House Museum photo.

Above left: John Snyder's barn in the late 1880s provided storage for hay and grain as well as a haven for cattle and horses. Photo courtesy of Lucille Kendall.

Left: The sea of pasture land shown here in the 1890s had been covered with thousands of homes and Interstate 280 a century later. Hidden in the trees on the left , adjacent to Permanente Creek, is the Snyder ranch headquarters– home, barns, winery, distillery and blacksmith shop. Photo courtesy of Lucille Kendall.

2

TRAINS, MANES AND AUTOMOBILES

BY ROY LAVE

Most cities of the world owe their beginnings to a transportation mode — first rivers, then railroads, and today, highways. The three creeks that traverse Los Altos defined spatial relationships, provided geographic milestones for the Ohlone Indians as well as convenient home and burial sites (a substantial find of Ohlone artifacts occurred in 1971 on the site of Creekside Oaks) and yielded fish and game for food. But, since the creeks were not navigable, the earliest residents of the Los Altos area got around on foot.

Los Altos was probably first seen by European explorers from horseback. The horse also provided the first form of public "mass" transit pulling stage coaches from Mountain View via El Monte Avenue and Moody Road to the Coast. An important stage stop was at Hidden Villa. The horse remained the major form of individual transportation until the early 1900s when the railroad and the newly introduced automobile relegated horses to recreational uses, an important role they continue to play in contemporary life.

Los Altos began its journey to becoming a community in 1906, when the Interurban Electric Railroad (I.E.R.) bought 100 acres of land between Palo Alto and Mountain View. A year later, the Southern Pacific Railroad purchased the 100 acres from the I.E.R. for the purpose of, in the words of Paul Shoup, who would become SP president, "locating a town in the vicinity of what is now Los Altos, to serve as a depot for the proposed Southern Pacific route." A branch of the steam driven Southern Pacific main line between San Francisco and Los Angeles was built through Los Altos and the West Santa Clara Valley to a connection with the existing branch line from San Jose and Santa Cruz. A parallel track ran between Palo Alto and West Valley for the Peninsular Railway Company, an electric commuter line owned by Southern Pacific. Both railroads opened the lands of Los Altos to homesites for those who would commute to San Francisco and to those who would escape the city for a country retreat. The rail station on First Street near Main Street preserves the appointments of the building erected in 1912-13 and still identifies the heart of the commercial center for Los Altos.

Map below reprinted from *Tracks, Tires & Wires* published by Interurban Press, 1981.

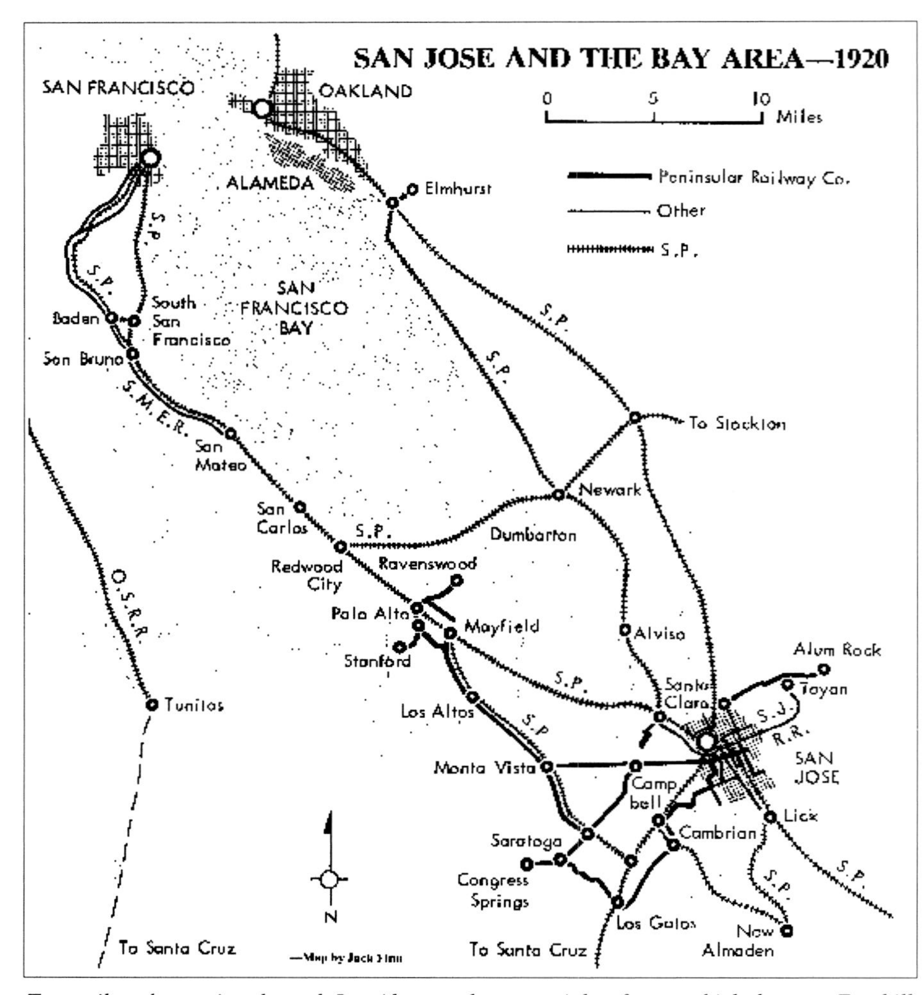

Two railroads running through Los Altos on the same right-of-way which became Foothill Expressway. The Southern Pacific steam train, a branch from the mainline San Francisco to San Jose, ran through Los Altos to Santa Cruz from around 1908 until 1958–known to some as the "Suntan Special." The electric Peninsular Railway Company (owned by Southern Pacific) provided service from Mayfield in Palo Alto to Los Gatos and San Jose from about 1910 to 1933, finally losing the battle to declining demand and the more flexible gasoline powered buses.

About the same time as the train made commuting to jobs north of the community attractive, automobile ownership began the growth that would ultimately replace both the horse and the train as the dominant form of transportation. The car brought to Los Altos filling stations and repair garages, among the first businesses in town.

Today roads define the spatial relation-

Steam train service to Los Altos was inaugurated in 1908 when 16 coaches filled with prospective buyers were brought to enjoy a barbecue as a land sale promotion device. This service became popular for commuting to San Francisco but ultimately declined and was discontinued in 1958. The engine pictured is in front of the powerhouse which was on First Street near where Safeway now stands. The powerhouse was built to provide power to the electric Peninsular Railway passenger service, the companion to the trains. The powerhouse also provided a boost to Los Altos, in the words of the Los Altos correspondent of the Palo Alto Times, "With the advent of this line will come electric lighting to our little town." History House Museum photo.

ships in the city much as the creeks did for the Ohlone. The major business district is called the downtown triangle because it is bounded on three sides by San Antonio Road, Edith Avenue and Foothill Expressway. Reliance on the automobile makes possible the low density residential character of Los Altos. It also causes the traffic congestion on both our local streets and the Foothill Expressway, itself made possible by the rail right-of-way it now covers.

Denial of the importance of the automobile may have motivated the long standing unofficial disdain for curbs and gutters in Los Altos which has been terminated by current ordinances requiring these enhancements. While the automobile may not be the most important factor in the lives of Los Altans, the care and feeding of cars consumes a significant portion of city government attention. Considerable time and emotion in City Council meetings are devoted to parking and traffic issues as citizens express their desire for unfettered use of streets except those in front of their houses.

What's ahead? Will BART traverse Los Altos? Will driverless autos hum along Foothill Expressway? Or will the horse make a comeback? □

Right: Before the permanent station was built at First and Main Streets, two box cars served as the station and the post office, after serving the same purpose in Palo Alto. The picture looks to the east and features the oak tree that continued to stand at the center of Main Street just before the Foothill Expressway intersection. No doubt in rebellion to being surrounded by paving, the tree died in 1970 and was replaced by the Canary Island Pine that stands in its place today. History House Museum photo.

Right: Three modes of early transportation that are still used today are shown in front of Shoup Hall above Robinson's Grocery (right), now a bank, and Eschenbruecher Hardware (left). Although the vehicles have changed, and the car is the dominant mode of transportation, bikes and horses are still a part of life in Los Altos and are joined by more modern modes of skateboards and roller blades. History House Museum photo.

Opposite page, top: Even in their demise, railroads contributed to modern transportation by providing the right of way that became Foothill Expressway in 1964. The first permanent rail station continues to enhance today's town. After years of idleness after train service was terminated in 1958, the station became a restaurant in 1962, then a savings and loan, and is now an antiques shop. The facade shown in the 1913 picture facing south to the tracks was reversed to face First Street when the building was converted to a restaurant. History House Museum photo.

Opposite page, bottom: After a train ride to Stanford, 125 Los Altans are proudly saluting their home town at a celebration of the opening of the Peninsular Railway line between Palo Alto and Los Altos on February 26, 1910. The new service was provided by five new cars, the "Big Reds" numbered 100, 101, 102, 103 and 104. San Jose Historical Museum photo.

ARE FROM
OS ALTOS

Map, above: The Peninsular Railway in 1915 provided service with multiple stops in Los Altos, including El Monte, Springer Road, Loyola and Grant Road. From Tracks, Tires & Wires, *published by Interurban Press, 1981.*

Dual railroad tracks once cut through Los Altos–the electric line on the left side, the Southern Pacific steam line on the right. The hill cut on the left can be seen as one drives north on Foothill Expressway from Main Street to Arastradero Road. J.C. Gordon photo from Wilbur C. Whittaker and Henry E. Morse Jr. Collection.

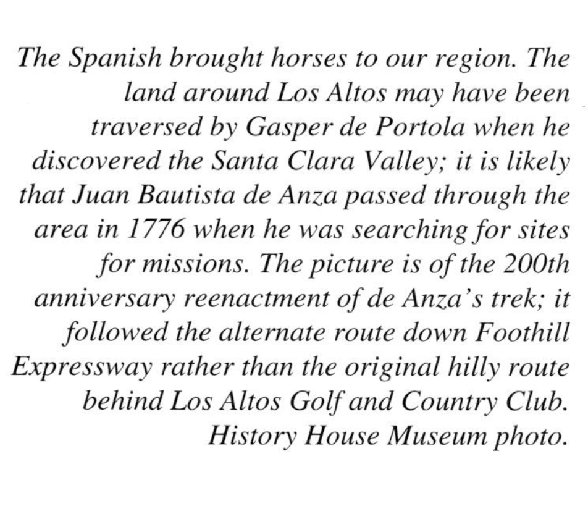

The Spanish brought horses to our region. The land around Los Altos may have been traversed by Gasper de Portola when he discovered the Santa Clara Valley; it is likely that Juan Bautista de Anza passed through the area in 1776 when he was searching for sites for missions. The picture is of the 200th anniversary reenactment of de Anza's trek; it followed the alternate route down Foothill Expressway rather than the original hilly route behind Los Altos Golf and Country Club. History House Museum photo.

Above: Los Altos might have been the San Jose of the Silicon Valley if the 1930s Isenberg "hayfield" airstrip off Fremont Road in Los Altos Hills had grown and attracted commercial flights. The Waco bi-plane attracted curious onlookers. Photo from the Florence Fava Collection, courtesy of Marjorie Kellogg-Van Rheeden.

Left: As a condition of abandoning the electric train service on the Mayfield cutoff, the State Railroad Commission (now the Public Utilities Commission) required that Peninsular Railway operate buses on the old electric route between Palo Alto, Los Altos, Loyola Corners, Monta Vista, Cupertino and Meridian Corners to San Jose. A Mayfair bus is shown here on First Street in 1960 with the Copeland Building (Arno's Restaurant in 1992) in the background. More extensive bus service came to town in 1973 when the county took over all private bus lines. Photo by Harre W. Demoro.

Bottom left: In contrast to the more elaborate station downtown, the Springer Station, shown in a 1949 photo appeared as a lonely outpost in the country. Photo from Lorin Silleman Collection.

Both Interstate 280 and Foothill Expressway have made Los Altos and Los Altos Hills a popular home for Silicon Valley executives, providing access to jobs from a community that has managed to maintain a geographic separation from the commercial sprawl that characterizes neighboring communities. Although highways can make towns, they can also break towns in two. The illustration shows an alternative route considered for Interstate 280, which was ultimately built farther west and south in the foothills. The first route chosen would have destroyed much of the charm of the downtown area of Los Altos. Photo reprinted from the book Los Altos Hills: The Colorful Story *by Florence Fava.*

UNIVERSITY AVE.
EL MONTE AVE.
PALM AVE.
1
1
1

3

A City Grows A Government

BY MARY VAN TAMELEN

WAR!

Make Los Altos a borough of Mountain View,
—urges Mountain View Shopping News

Mountain View and certain outside interests have united to prevent the people of Los Altos from solving their own problems.
They have misrepresented, misled, confused.
They will stop at nothing to defeat incorporation.

Mountain View "Carpet Baggers" Fighting Incorporation!

Should Los Altos Incorporate ?

Don't Be Fooled By Half Truths

Misrepresentation - Misquotation

"We want to incorporate to keep from becoming a city," said A. Watson Conner, later to become the first mayor of Los Altos. Fear of intense development and the possible annexation of adjoining lands by Mountain View fueled the desire of residents to form a town and wrest control from the Board of Supervisors in San Jose.

Volunteers drew maps, checked records, prepared voting lists, set boundaries and urged incorporation. On November 25, 1952, the vote count was 2,138 in favor, 1,906 opposed. On December 1, after certification by the Board of Supervisors at noon, the affixing of the State Seal in Sacramento at 3:30 p.m., and the swearing in of the new council, the first City Council meeting began at 6 p.m. Conner; Burt H. Riggs, retired rancher; Clarence O. Witt, retired mechanical engineer; Joseph W. Fortunato, engineer, and George Estill, airline manager, met in a borrowed music room in the San Antonio School.

The first items of business included emergency legislation to contract for fire protection. Eileen Verhoye was appointed city clerk, without pay, and Gardner Bullis, city attorney, also without pay. Later Joseph McClellend was sworn in as first police chief, a planning commission was appointed and Joseph Salameda was hired as a building inspector. The Los Altos Garbage Company proposed that it pay the city a franchise fee to collect garbage-the city's first income!

Merchants planted the trees on Main Street during a Sunday afternoon "tree-planting bee." The public works department began with a pickup truck, a shovel and pick, and the employment of Arthur Bisgaard. The city was in business. The incorporation of Los Altos led the way for other cities—Saratoga, Cupertino, Milpitas and Monte Sereno soon followed the example set by Los Altos. And in 1956 residents in the adjoining hills voted 424-339 to incorporate to protect their one-acre residential, rural zoning. Proposed names for the new town included Purissima or Toyon, but the working title, Los Altos Hills, stuck.

Through the years, the city government has met the challenge of floods, traffic congestion, parking needs, sewage treatment, fire and police services, solid waste disposal, droughts, recycling, two-story home controversies, gas-powered leaf blowers and senior citizen concerns. Councils, staff and commissions continue to rise to all occasions, maintaining a sense of community for all to enjoy.

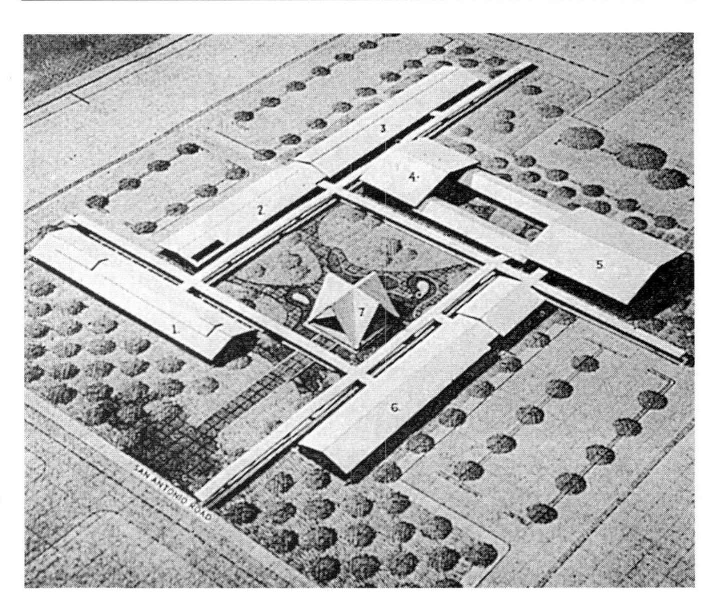

Top: Posters from the incorporation movement in 1952 set the tone for a highly contested election. At the time of incorporation, Los Altos was the 11th city in the county and fourth largest. Now there are 15 cities and only three are smaller. From Foothill Focus.

Bottom: In the late 1950s, Ernest J. Kump Associates proposed a civic center that included: 1) City Hall offices; 2) art center; 3) police department; 4) youth center gymnasium; 5) community center auditorium; 6) library; 7) town hall council chambers, surrounded by a shallow pool. From Foothill Focus

Above: Aerial view of Los Altos and Los Altos Hills in the 1950s. The Hillview and San Antonio Schools are in the left foreground; orchards reach almost as far as the eye can see into the hills. The large home in the orchard in the center foreground was built by J. Gilbert Smith in 1905. It is now the History House Museum. History House Museum photo.

Left: The first city council and city staff in front of City Hall on First Street; 1st Row: Councilmen C.O. Will, George Estill, Mayor A. Watson Conner, Councilmen Burt Riggs and Joseph Fortunato; 2nd Row: Police Chief Joseph McClelland, City Clerk John Hope, Building Inspector Joe Salameda. 3rd Row: City Clerk Eileen Verhoye, Patrolmen Roland Renshaw, Bernard Diller, Kenneth Young, Chris Brett and Charles Demars, Street Maintenanceman Joe Ryan, City Clerk Secretary Mary Penninton, Building Department Secretary Portia Chamberlain. History House Museum photo.

3

A City Grows A Government

> ***"Federal governments have the money, state governments have the authority, and local governments have the problems."***
>
> ***—Mayor Roy Lave, 1977***

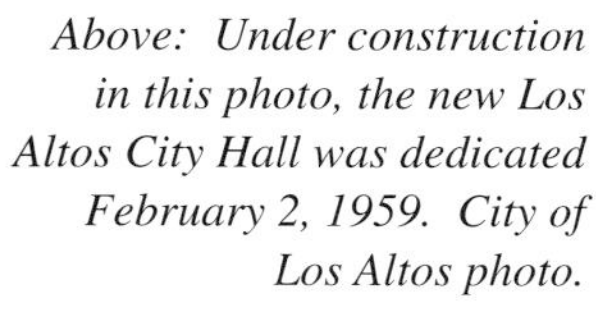

Above: Under construction in this photo, the new Los Altos City Hall was dedicated February 2, 1959. City of Los Altos photo.

Right: Los Altos City Hall with staff in 1972. Left to right: Yosh Hirotsuka, Jack Lovell, Jim Dozier, Gail Nobel, Yvonne Zirzow (front), Bob Workman, Ron Gruenwald, Dave Donahue, Jim Carter, Annie Thomson, George Sanregret, Carol Hoffman (front), Joan Weepie, Sherry Lambach, Linda Workman, Dave Hansen and Lucy James. City of Los Altos photo.

Top left: Downtown charm was enhanced with the installation of new lampposts in 1967.

Top right: Storm drains are installed throughout the city.

Above left: Los Altos fire-fighting equipment, 1920. History House Museum photo.

Above right: Fire department equipment in 1992. Photo by Christiane Dubrelle.

Left: Los Altos built a sewage treatment plant on city owned property at the end of San Antonio Road in 1957. This was later abandoned after Los Altos joined with Palo Alto and Mountain View in the use of the Tri-City plant. History House Museum photo.

"In politics we shall be Republican, for it's in our blood and we can't help it–but this will not prevent us from being fair friends with the Democrats; in fact, we are of the opinion that Santa Clara County has too many Republicans to be in a healthy state of existence, so we can but consistently hope for more Democrats that honors may be more evenly divided, and enough Democrats kept in the field to make a decent fight. Our religion shall be as broad as the ocean and as wide as the land, and our creed shall be 'success to Los Altos,' the Crown of the Peninsula and the Dream of the Gods!"

Editorial by Walter A. Clark in his inaugural issue of the Los Altos Star, August 5, 1908, announcing the kind of community that was being proposed.

Top right: First police force of the newly incorporated city being sworn in: Charles Gilbert DeMar, Bennie B. Dillard, Roland R. Renshaw and Thomas C. Letcher.

Center right: Call for police action at Loyola Corners in 1955.

Above: Making history in 1990: Lucy Carlton became Los Altos' first female police chief. Photo by Marjorie Kellogg-Van Rheeden.

Bottom: First police cars on Main Street. Roland Renshaw, later police chief, poses with the cars under an oak tree, since removed because of disease. History House Museum photo.

Left: Engineering department in 1988 celebrates completion of the Hetch-Hechy bike path over Adobe Creek, off Los Altos Avenue. Left to right: Phyllis Semple, Dave Donahue, Daphne Siegert, Lyn Lavery, Ed Jackson, Bruce Bane, Brian Keating and Yosh Hirotsuka. Los Altos Engineering Department Photo.

Above: Los Altos Hills opens a new section of its extensive pathway system in honor of Artemas Ginzton in 1991. She accepts the scissors from Sid Hubbard, Mayor. Barbara Tryon, vice-mayor is on the right.

Top: Gallery of Los Altos mayors 1952-1992 covers a wall in the City Hall. Photo by Marjorie Kellogg-Van Rheeden.

Above middle: 1972 Planning Commission , left to right: Jim Powers, Fred Pfleger, Paul Noble, Larry Madsen, Roy Krell and Roger Eng.

Above: Los Altos Hills added City Council Chambers to its Town Hall on Fremont Road. Mayor Stanley Grabowski turned the first shovel of soil, watched by architect Bill Minckley and Councilman Robert Cheney (kneeling) and left to right: Joe Semonini, Councilwoman Diana Miller, Karl Fovenyersy and City Engineer Alex Russell. History House Museum photo.

4

EVOLVING HOME STYLES—BARNS TO BEDROOMS

BY MARK SANDOVAL

Los Altos has an abundance of homes of diverse architectural styles popularized by Bay Area architects and builders from the late 1800s to the present. The result is a wonderful and unique mix of residential neighborhoods and building styles, reflecting traditional values and pride shared by all who make up the local communities.

Before the turn of the 20th century, typical wood farm houses, similar to the one immortalized in the painting by Grant Wood, "American Gothic," with their covered verandahs, turned support posts and simple painted wood exterior, dotted the rural landscape of what is now Santa Clara Valley.

The early settlers of the Valley brought with them a mix of building vernaculars reflecting eastern styles popular during this time: Greek, Classic, Gothic, Italian Revival and Federal styles, to name a few.

With the advent of the Southern Pacific Railroad expansion and the population migration south from San Francisco, a new development pattern began to emerge, the railroad suburb. Homes with their wood clapboard sheathed exteriors generally employed the use of simple hip roofs to create a less imposing, yet more formal base to which architectural components could be attached. Mostly adorned with simple Classic Revival architectural embellishments, these homes were built on a rectangular floor plan, incorporating a raised porch and positioning a small attic or partial second floor dormer above the front entry door.

The bungalow, a term derived from the word Banglas (a form of housing found in the Bangal Province of India), and the Bay Area's version of the Craftsman style home, popularized by the Pasadena architects Green and Green, was introduced to the Peninsula in the early part of this century. Most of the homes surviving from this period in Los Altos were built between 1905 and 1915. Typically these woodsy homes made use of natural materials such as stone and redwood siding.

After the 1906 San Francisco earthquake, a strong preference for stucco and masonry buildings arose bringing the emergence of the Mission Revival. The style was an easy and inexpensive way for a developer to decorate a simple box by adding a stucco arch and a row of Spanish tile. This style was

The sleepy town of Los Altos as seen from an aerial photo taken in 1947. From the earliest beginnings, Los Altos planners and residents have tried to promote development patterns that maintain the character of its semi-rural heritage.

Above: The early home styles introduced to the Bay Area and Santa Clara Valley were from pattern books which promoted a collection of styles. Popular during this period were Gothic Revival and Italianate designs which are exemplified in the home of John "49er" Snyder, built about 1860 near Grant Road and Foothill Expressway. Photo courtesy of Lucille Kendall.

Left: The Farnsworth/Myers home was rehabilited in 1989/90 and became part of a planned unit development at the end of Rinconada Court. It has been designated a local Los Altos landmark. Photo by Christiane Dubrulle.

short lived (about 10 years) and eventually evolved in the '20s and '30s into the Spanish Revival.

Between 1919 and 1932 an unusual building style appeared, promoted by Bay Area architects such as Yelland and Comstock. These homes and cottages took on a childlike quality often miniaturized in scale, and borrowed from European Medieval styles to evoke a certain mood rather than depicting any particular period or style.

The Post War period led to radical patterns in residential housing. New styles emerged to promote mass production housing for the returning G.I.s. Bay Area architects such as William Wurster began to turn their attention to other architectural forms. The new low-profile utilitarian-looking structures with their vertical and horizontal board siding and extended eaves, emphasized a simple carpenter approach to home building. Often labeled as "shanty-style," these structures would evolve into the California Ranch. This new form received national acceptance and became the single most important residential style in Los Altos and Los Altos Hills.

Santa Clara Valley then witnessed the development of a modern regional approach to home design. Joseph Eichler with the assistance of architects such as Ashen & Allen, Jones & Emmons, and Claude Oakland, produced innovative home designs. These originally were designed for the mass market housing industry, and later were expanded and adapted to the custom, single-family home market. These often boxy and sometimes austere wood clad homes would incorporate the use of exposed concrete slab floors, entrances through atrium courtyards and large areas of glass to create a visual openness and connection with the outdoors.

Today Los Altos, Los Altos Hills and the rest of the Bay Area are experiencing new patterns of development. There is a return to more traditional imported building vernaculars from other parts of the country. Eclectic Traditional, Mediterranean and Country French are generally a collection of many styles incorporated and synthesized into one. Although many of the early homes in this style appear imposing and awkwardly excessive with detail and roof complexity, the later homes which are generally professionally designed have removed the brash and inappropriate detailing in favor of a more pure and clear architectural style. □

Top: Homes located along Orange Avenue are shown in this photo taken in 1908 from a brochure promoting Los Altos by the Altos Land Company. These modestly styled homes were typical of those built during the early development of Los Altos. History House Museum photo.

Center: The Formway home built about 1910 typifies many of the early pattern book homes in the area. Simple and straight forward, these homes clearly reflected the traditional values of the early settlers. History House Museum photo.

Bottom: One of the earliest tract developments in Los Altos was Chester Manor built about 1942. These modest homes were typical of those built during the early Bay Area post-war home building boom. Photo by Don Roper.

Top: Lantarnam Hall, also known as Morgan Manor and later the Ford Country Day School, was built in 1914-15 and is representative of the unique estates constructed on the Peninsula after the San Francisco earthquake and fire. Most were elaborate and grand in scale and depicted another place and time rather than referencing any particular regional or local building vernaculars. Photo by Marjorie Kellogg-Van Rheeden.

Above: Enter the 1950s and the California Ranch! Use of embellishment along eaves, diamond shaped windows, mini hay lofts or dovecotes, cupolas and wagon wheels were favorite details of merchant builders. Photo by Don Roper.

Above, left: Joseph Eichler, once a butter and egg salesman, became a home builder during the late 1940s. Examples of his boxy, wood clad styles are located on Parsons Way. Photo by Don Roper.

Left: Almendra Lane in Los Altos is a 1990 development that reintroduces the basement as an integral part of the site planning design. Photo by Don Roper.

5

Commerce Without Industry

BY CONRAD HEINTZELMAN

Los Altos—a city without industry. There are no factories, industrial plants or large farms. However, this was not always the case.

Early in the development of this section of Santa Clara County, agriculture dominated. Grain and dairy farming thrived prior to 1900. In this century, grain and hay fields evolved into irrigated cash crops of apricots, cherries, cut flowers, walnuts, prunes and plums. With its Mediterranean climate and rich soil, Los Altos was a desirable place to raise a crop and a family.

Land developers, with the assistance of the railroad, promoted Los Altos as a place to be relished, the "crown of the peninsula," with summer homes for San Franciscans and as primary residences. Land became more valuable as the community became more a place to live than a place to work.

As aviation, aerospace, electronics, and all facets of the computer industry and internet services flourished in the last half of the 20th Century in what had become Silicon Valley, Los Altos and Los Altos Hills became "hometown" to hundreds of executives, engineers and management personnel. As the population grew, the commercial districts expanded.

Los Altos has seven distinct retail areas containing a strong mix of services: real estate, medical, legal, accounting, banking, printing, publishing, travel, beauty, software development and internet providers. In addition to the services, retailers offer antiques, clothing, housewares, plants, flowers, groceries, office supplies, videos, books and gifts. Dozens of popular restaurants satisfy the needs of residents and neighbors alike.

Numerous commercially oriented and sponsored events occur throughout the year. The annual Art and Wine Festival, sponsored by the Los Altos Village Association, has evolved into one of the largest festivals in Northern California. LAVA also supports the Breakfast-With-Santa Children's Show, Easter Egg Hunt, the holiday tree lighting night and a scholarship fund. The Rancho Roundup Pancake Breakfast raises money for PTA. The Los Altos Chamber of Commerce sponsors a fall festival, annual golf tournament and publishes a colorful guide to Los Altos each year.

Los Altos is proud to be hometown to the prestigious David and Lucile Packard Foundation. By the end of the 20th Century, the foundation was among the top three largest foundations in the nation and the city's largest non-governmental employer.

Los Altos may be a city without industry, but it is filled with an industrious population and a business community that means business. □

Top: Casual parking style was the order of the day on Main Street, 1924.

Bottom: Chartered in 1919, First National Bank opened with $25,000 in capital. In the 1940s Guy Shoup, holding the flag, and pharmacist Sammy Kahn at his left were among the directors. Photo by Studio D'Art.

Above: Grain and dairy farms covered hundreds of acres of what became Los Altos and Los Altos Hills in the late 1800s and into the 20th Century. The view is across the tracks from Loyola corners about 1920.

Right: Apricots became a major cash crop in Los Altos once low cost water was available for irrigation. The annual ritual of "cot cutting and drying" involved hundreds of people and created this familiar scene.

Below right: Formway Machine Shop on Almond Avenue was Los Altos' only factory. Here the Wizard Walnut Huller was invented and manufactured.

Below: A 1908 real estate ad in the Los Altos Star makes a bold prediction. Photos on page courtesy of History House Museum.

You Should Buy A Lot in Los Altos

Without question Los Altos is destined to become the best residence town in the Santa Clara Valley. Lots are 50 x 142 feet in size. Terms, $50 down and balance $10 per month. Each lot has cement sidewalk, cement curb, alley, shade trees, water and sewer. Prices are $400, $425 and $450 for inside lots, $650 for corner lots. Title perfect. The present train service puts Los Altos only 57 minutes from San Francisco. For full information address or call upon

WALTER A. CLARK
GENERAL AGENT

Los Altos, California

Agencies:
Jos. H. Rucker & Co., 49 Post St., San Francisco.
T. C. Barnett, 27 N. First St. San Jose.
H. A. Thompson, Palo Alto.

5

Commerce Without Industry

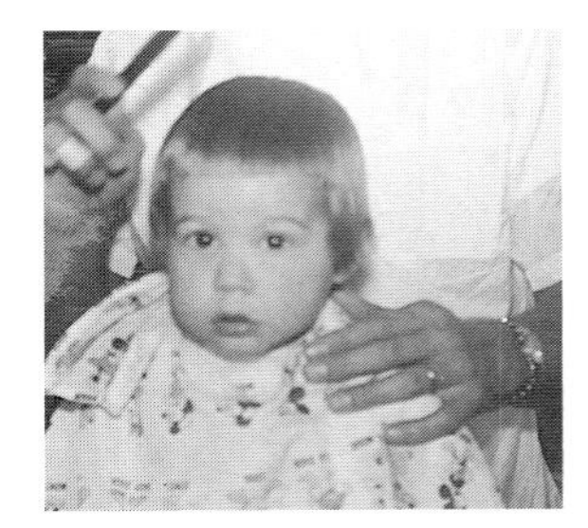

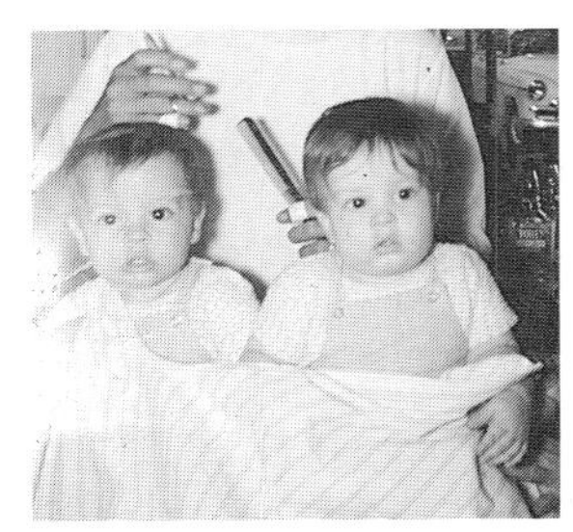

Above: Al's Barber Shop on Main Street is the oldest continuously operating downtown Los Altos business. With partner Louis Piro, Al Galedrige (upper far right in 1948 photo) has clipped several generations of Los Altans. First haircut for Maridee Huston (top), whose parents Jack and Bobbie Huston were co-owners of the Russell-Huston Clothing Store. Twins Mitch and Steve Garvich got first haircuts in 1954. Their father, Chuck Garvich,was a long time Los Altos Post Office employee. Photos courtesy of Al Galedrige.

Right: One of the most popular events staged in Los Altos fills both State and Main Streets for two full days each summer: The Art and Wine Festival sponsored by the Downtown Village Association. Photo courtesy of Jane Reed

Below: Foothill Expressway underpass at Loyola Corners was constructed in 1965 after the demise of the railroad.

Above: Main Street 1992 is a tree-lined oasis for shoppers that has maintained the friendly, quaint atmosphere established a half century earlier. Photo by Ellen M. Banner.

Above: Main Street 1940. Downtown Los Altos was captured from a Navy blimp by Captain Stan Garbranski of Moffett Field. He was owner of Los Altos Sport Shop as well. In this pre-World War overview note that stores were clustered between First Street and Third Street along Main; sidewalks for State Street (extreme right) have been installed, but State seems to still be gravel; wide alleys parallel to Main Street would later become the parking plazas; the train station and railroad tracks were still heavily used; two large oaks flank the train station; the art deco style Los Altos Pharmacy building at Main and Second Streets was such a classic it has survived to become LeBoulanger in 1992; tightly packed cars in front of the retail stores meant finding a parking place was just as difficult then as 50 years later. Photo courtesy of Al Galedridge.

Below: The Chamber of Commerce building at University and Main Street was designed in 1961 by Los Altos architect Goodwin Steinberg. Photo by Christiane Dubrelle.

Above: 1954 view of Rancho Shopping Center. Built in 1951, Rancho is a planned shopping center made up of Spanish ranch-style shops of adobe and brick construction with heavy shake roofs. Photo by Studio D'Art.

Center: Two dedicated community servants as well as Rancho merchants: Troy Underwood is former owner of Rancho Hardware; Dave Leary owns Murphys Pizza and TV Associates. Both are former presidents of Rancho Merchants Associates.

Below: (left to right) Enduring landmarks–Foodland on Los Altos Avenue, Mac's Tea Room on Main Street and DiMartini's fruit and vegetable stand--still a favorite stop for busy travellers on San Antonio Road. Photos by Conrad Heintzelman.

Right: 1957. El Camino Real and San Antonio Road, looking southwest. Sears and large parking area are in center foreground. The Old Plantation Inn is visible at the intersection of El Camino Real and San Antonio–in 1992 Village Court shopping area. Photo by Pacific Aerial Surveys.

Center: Krikor & Vehanoush Boursalian–Shoemakers at Village Court, 1992. Photo by Marjorie Kellogg-Van Rheeden.

Below: Memorable events below: The October 17, 1989, earthquake made a mess of Midtown Market (below left); the Loyola Corners Farmers Market (center below) is popular on weekends in the 1990s; Pete Harman studies wall mural of Colonel Sanders on his Kentucky Fried Chicken store on First Street. LAH resident Harman owned the very first KFC franchise in the nation. The mural was painted by Jan Meyer and Caroline Peterson.

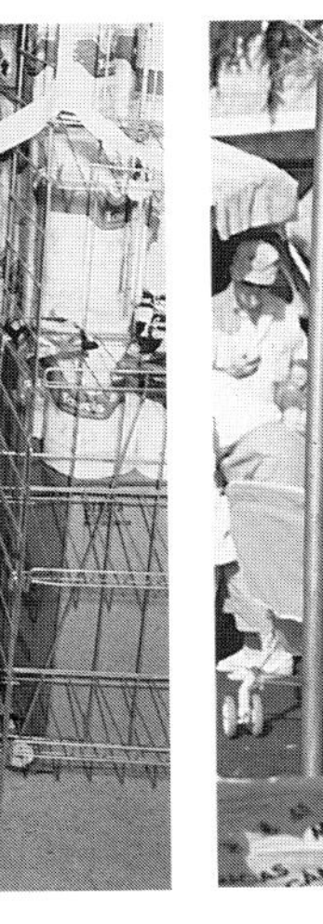

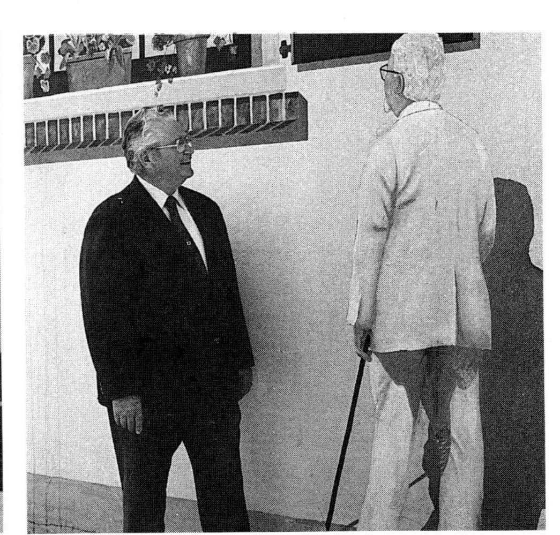

6

SCHOOLS: HEARTBEAT OF THE COMMUNITY

BY JEAN NEWTON

Since 1908 when the first official public school classes were held upstairs above the grocery store in the Shoup Building on Main Street, Los Altos schools have provided the heartbeat for our community. Traditionally serving as a gathering place for citizens, our neighborhood schools are not only recognized as exceptional educational centers for the future leaders of tomorrow, but have become a source of spirit and dedication that binds our communities together.

The concept of neighborhood schools–long recognized as a significant ingredient in the academic success of our local public school system–was established in the 1950's when San Antonio School, the one large community school in operation at San Antonio Road and Hillview Avenues, was declared seismically unsafe for students. Ardis G. Egan, then superintendent of schools, spearheaded a campaign that resulted in the construction of 14 new schools during his 21-year term, as he watched the elementary district grow from 350 to more than 6,000 students. Neighborhood schools became the cornerstone of our community, creating an important link for school, business and community members, and contributing to the serene, yet spirited and caring, hometown flavor that is so unique to Los Altos.

1957 aerial photo shows San Antonio Grammar School (right center) with then new Hillview School nearby. The San Antonio School building was razed in 1972 because it did not meet earthquake safety standards. Photo courtesy of Pacific Aerial Surveys of Oakland.

Cooperation between the city and the schools dates back to December 5, 1952, when school board minutes—just four days after the incorporation of the City of Los Altos—show Los Altos School District board members Georgina P. Blach, Richard S. Bullis and Charles C. Manger approving "a loan of twelve chairs along with a desk and a chair" and granting a request "for use of a room every two weeks until such time as the city can provide a meeting place."

With one of the best public school systems in the state of California, Los Altos has always offered area residents excellent educational choices with

Above: For two years, from 1908 to 1910, the two-story Shoup Building housed the very first Los Altos public school classes, where one teacher taught all eight grades upstairs above the grocery store.

Below: In the early 1950s, Los Altos students attended high school in Mountain View on Castro Street until Los Altos High School on Almond Avenue was completed in 1955. Chester F. Awalt High School was built in the early 1960s on Truman Avenue, but after the Castro Street high school closed its doors in 1982, Awalt's name was changed to Mountain View High School and students from the two towns merged to attend high school there and at Los Altos High School.

Above: First public school class consisting of all eight grades taken beside the Shoup Building in 1909. History House Museum photo.

Below: The first school to be built in Los Altos, San Antonio School, was also called Los Altos Grammar School. Once located at the corner of Hillview Avenue and San Antonio Road, the building accommodated grades K-8 in one large community school. This photo was taken after construction was completed in 1911 at a cost of $12,000. District officials closed San Antonio School in 1952, after earthquakes in Bakersfield and Tehachapi, because the structure did not meet the requirements of the Field Act (earthquake act) and was no longer safe to occupy. History House Museum photo.

Below: Class of 1922 , Los Altos Grammar School. History House Museum photo.

many parochial and private schools and a wide variety of nearby colleges and universities from which to choose.

Six public elementary schools are in operation—Almond, Bullis, Loyola, Oak, Springer and Santa Rita—and two junior high schools, Blach and Egan. A third junior high, Covington School, built in1950 served for several years as offices for the Los Altos School District. In early 2000 it is scheduled to reopen as an elementary school to satisfy the population changes. Los Altos School District Schools have been named California Distinguished Schools and all are included in the list of the Top 100 Schools in California.

At the high school level, Los Altos High School and Mountain View High School, also California Distinguished Schools, serve Los Altos, Los Altos Hills and Mountain View students. Some Los Altos and Los Altos Hills young people attend school in the Palo Alto Unified School District at Lucile Nixon Elementary School, J.L. Stanford Middle School and Gunn High School; in the Cupertino Union School District at Montclair Elementary School and Cupertino Junior High; or in the Fremont Union High School District at Homestead High School.

Several private schools, both parochial and secular, are located in Los Altos. Catholic schools include St. Simon and St. Nicholas for grades K-8 while St. Francis High School serves grades 9-12. Pinewood, a college preparatory school offers classes for

Top: Purissima School students in1918. From the left and indicated by the boxes above their heads: Leonard Burnhart, Jules Matteis, Lester Brubaker, Emile Larrus and Oscar Holm.

Above: Overview of Bullis-Purissima School. Faced with the reality of double sessions for elementary students during the 1950s, district officials would build new schools over the next 10 years to accommodate the post World War II baby boomers and to house almost 6,000 K-8 students by 1965.

Below: San Antonio Grammar School student body, grades one through eight in 1927. History House Museum photo.

Above: An elegant dining room becomes a classroom. Ford Country Day School, a prestigious private school opened in 1955 in Morgan Manor in Los Altos Hills—built in 1912 by Percy T. Morgan. Founded by John Carter Ford, the school was later owned by Brent Warner before its closure in1986. Photo courtesy of Marjorie Kellogg-Van Rheeden.

Right: John and Margaret Ford (1950) founded Ford Country Day School on Stonebrook Court in Los Altos Hills. Photo courtesy of Marjorie Kellogg-Van Rheeden.

students in Kindergarten through grade 12. Colleges and Universities close by include Foothill College in Los Altos Hills and De Anza College in Cupertino, both two-year community colleges, and three major universities, San Jose State University, Santa Clara University and Stanford University.

As centers for community cooperation, our schools act as a catalyst to bring people together. Concerned teachers help students discover the joy of learning, parents form life-long friendships through PTA, and community members take pride in knowing Los Altos schools play a significant and cohesive role as builders of a strong community. □

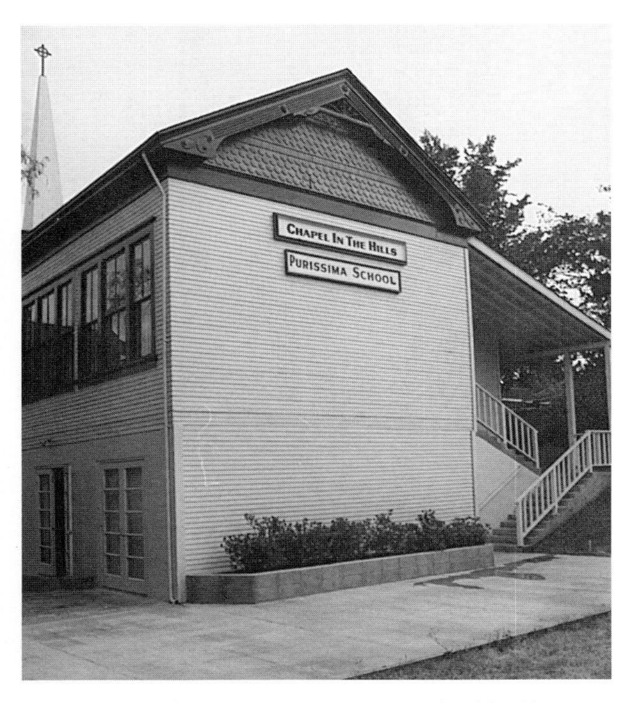

Above: Historic Purissima School building was converted to a church, Chapel In The Hills . Photo by Marjorie Kellogg-Van Rheeden.

Top right: 1952 –Students line up for a hot lunch served from the Almond Elementary School cafeteria. Photo courtesy of the Town Crier.

Center right: 1992–Proposition 13 and other state funding restrictions made cafeterias obsolete. Children bring brown bag lunches to eat on school picnic tables like these students from Almond Elementary School.

Right bottom: Second grader Christopher Jaworski learns how to read, write, and type with the computer program "Talking Fingers." Computer labs, a future dream in 1952, are a reality of the 1992 educational curriculum thanks in part to the donation of computer labs by the Los Altos Educational Foundation. Photo by Matt Durham.

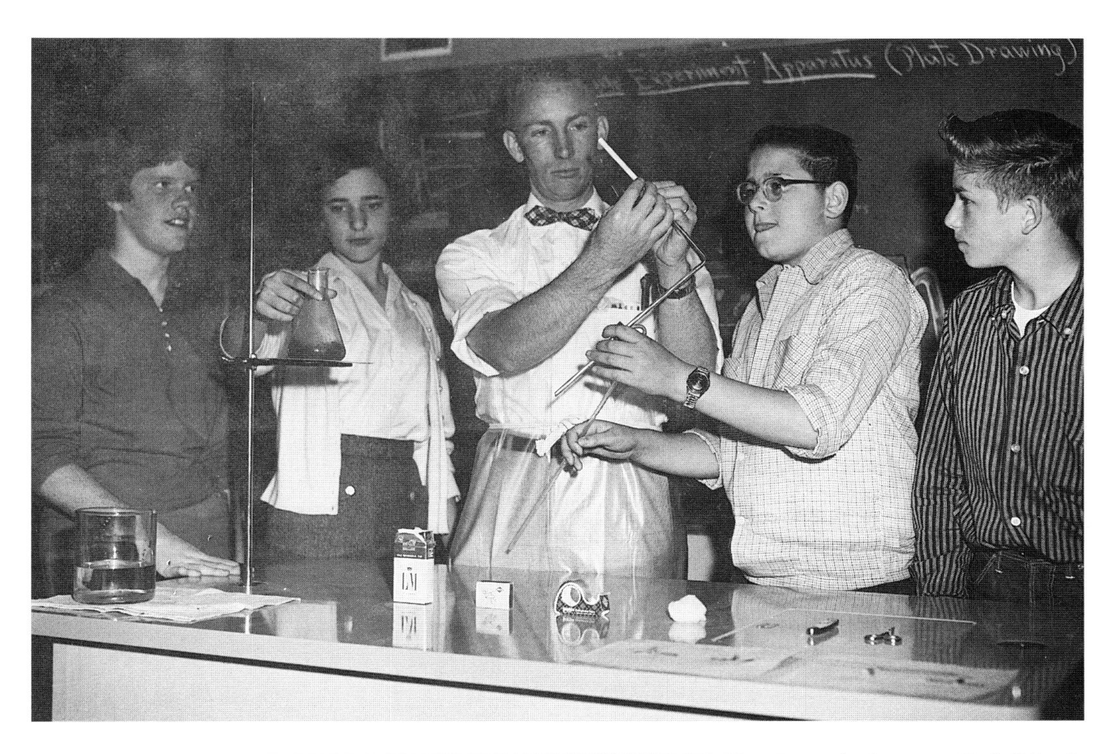

Top: Blach Junior High School students conduct a lab experiment during the 1950s with science teacher Earl Heusser.

Left: Mountain View High School in 1992. Students rally to express concern over controversial Rodney King verdict in Los Angeles. Photo by Melissa Marciano.

Below left: 1992 Los Altos High School Senior Class President Sam Chun and good friend Marvin Goodrich take time out from watching a band competition. Students from the cities of Mountain View, Los Altos and Los Altos Hills all come together under the umbrella of the Mountain View-Los Altos Union High School District at Mountain View and Los Altos High Schools, where a shared diversity fosters acceptance and understanding of all cultures. Photo by Kiley Schwehr.

Below right: Former after-school hangout—Clint's ice cream was famous throughout the Peninsula. Photo provided by Margaret Salameda, courtesy of Clint Roe. Photo by Studio D'Art.

7

Service Clubs

BY DICK FOUQUET

The history of service clubs in Los Altos reflects the cohesiveness and friendly spirit of the town. It's a tale of men and women using their talents and resources to help others and make Los Altos a better place to live.

Los Altos' first service club was the Kiwanis Club, founded in November 1947 by School Superintendent Ardis Egan, with Bert Schweitzer, Don Gordon and Wallace Stanley. Earlier that same year, these four organized the town's first annual Pet Parade. Kiwanis also sponsors annual Special Games for physically handicapped youth.

The Rotary Club of Los Altos was chartered in March, 1949, by Guy Shoup and a group from Mountain View Rotary. The club puts on the Fine Arts Show during Mayfest Weekend each year. Funds are used locally for scholarships, youth activities and many community benefit agencies. Sunset Rotary, an evening club, was organized in 1986 by a group of Los Altos Rotarians. The clubs have sponsored a Cub Scout pack, given several area youth Rotary Foundation scholarships for study abroad, participated in the Festival of Lights Parade and supported the Salvation Army.

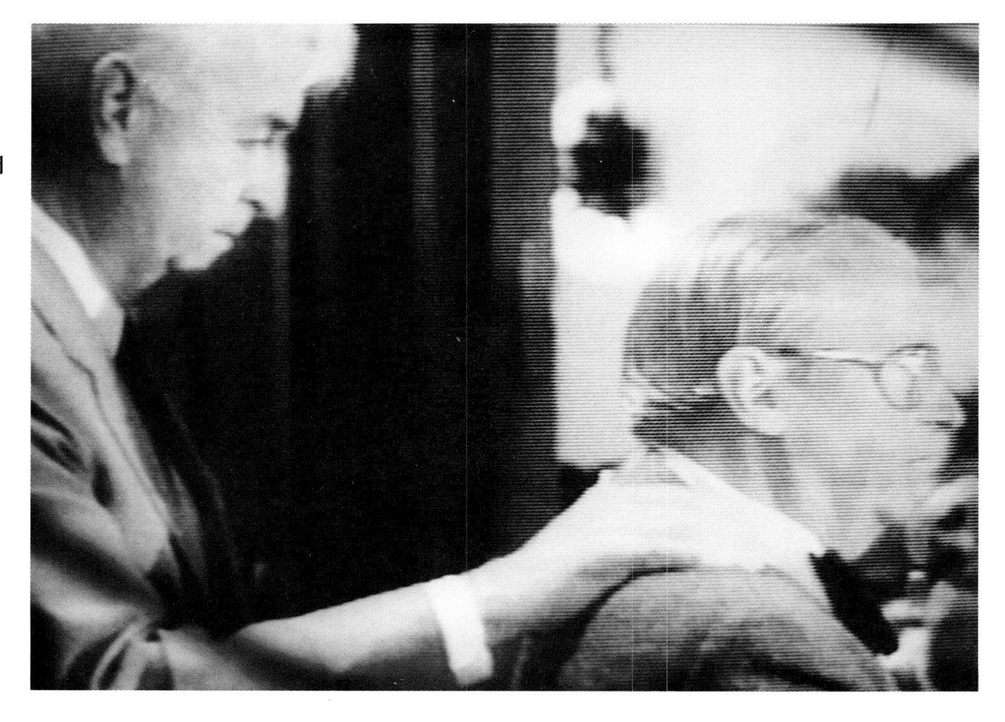

No doubt the most dramatic scene ever experienced at a service club anywhere was the day in 1989 that Los Altos businessman, Walt Singer, announced that he had AIDS. When the disease affected three members of the Los Altos Rotary, the club undertook a project in AIDS education and produced a video that has been seen by millions of families on national TV and has been honored with prestigious awards, including the George F. Peabody and cable TV's ACE awards. The video has been distributed to all 25,000 Rotary clubs worldwide. Here, in an emotional scene from the video, Club President Dude Angius, whose son Steve died from AIDS, comforts Singer as he explains how he contracted the virus from a blood transfusion four years earlier. Singer passed away in 1992. Town Crier photo by Matt Durham.

The Quota Club of Los Altos was started in 1949 by Fran Woodward, longtime dean of students at Los Altos High school. For many years the club provided scholarships for hearing impaired, supported battered women and child abuse centers and the local Senior Center. The Quota Club was discontinued in the mid 1990s.

The Los Altos Sertoma Club, founded in 1960, works to help speech and hearing disabled children. The club runs a Pancake Breakfast during Mayfest Weekend and a food booth at the July Art & Wine Festival. In the summer it also puts on fun family barbecues in Shoup Park the last Sunday of each month. These fund-raisers enable Sertoma to support the Jean Weingarten Peninsula Oral School for the Deaf and other local groups.

For 40 years, Los Altos had an active Lions Club founded in 1951

1999
LOS ALTOS SERVICE CLUBS

Kiwanis
Meets at noon on Tuesday, Mac's American Grill

Los Altos Rotary
Meets at noon on Thursday, Garden House

Los Altos Sunset Rotary
Meets at 7 p.m. on Tuesday, Mac's American Grill

Sertoma
Meets at 7:15 a.m. on Thursday, Lyons

Above: In 1966, the Los Altos Rotary Club solved a traffic flow problem at the intersection of State and Main Streets by creating a traffic island and planting a tree. Left to right: Jim Dozier, then City Finance Officer; Roland Renshaw, Chief of Police; and Ed Garrett, Manager of United California Bank. Photo supplied by Los Altos City Hall.

Center: The Rotary Tree at the intersection of State and Main Streets in 1992. The tree was removed in 1993 to make way for the new Community Plaza underwritten by Rotary. Photo by Dick Fouquet.

Left: in 1947, one of Kiwanis' charter members was Judge Paul Myers II.His grandson, Alex, was the 1992 President of Kiwanis. Two other grandsons,Chico and Jeff, were also members. Photo by Sheldon of Los Altos.

by Chuck Garvich, Frank Furuichi, Jack Norman and Bob Parrett. For most of those years, the Lions held a Flea Market during Mayfest to help support the Santa Clara Blind Center and the San Francisco Eye Foundation. Locally, club members were active boosters of youth, sponsoring a speech contest, scholarships and youth athletics. The club was disbanded in 1991, probably a victim of changing life styles that made the evening meeting time less popular.

During the 1960s, the Optimists Club's 35 members were dedicated to helping youth, notably supporting "Boysville," a summer camp for 400-500 boys from disadvantaged areas. Founding President Phil Packer was joined by other town leaders such as Dr. Mayfield Harris, Mort MacLeod, Wayne Miller, Dr. Frank White and Don Terhune. □

Top right: On a summer Sunday afternoon, Sertoma members, in aprons, left to right: Dick Whealan, Sandy Pakaski and Dick Sulloway serve up hamburgers and hot dogs to Los Altans in Shoup Park. Photo by Jim M'Guinness.

Above: Service clubs find many ways to serve their communities. Club president Don Terhune (left) and Mike Mansch of the Stanford Area Rotary Club stand at an I-280 sign that heralds one of the services their club provides.

Right center: Founders of Los Altos Rotary celebrate a new president in July 1952. Left to right: Neville "Bill" Williams, Charlie Helser, Guy Shoup and Larry Gentry.

Bottom: Some of the past presidents of Quota Club at a get-together. Back row, left to right: Vi Sullivan, Patti Williams, Jackie Wallace and Carol Tefft. Front row: Marie White, Audrey Fisher, Sherry Lambach and Arlene Lambach.

Above: Pets come in all sizes and shapes. This llama in the 1992 Pet Parade doesn't seem at all happy to be hoofing it down Main Street. Sheldon of Los Altos Photo.

Left: Pet Parades may look the same from year to year, but the town changes. In this 1976 picture, horses prance past the old Los Altos Theater on Main Street, now the home of The Works and Ligtelyn's Travel Agency. Murry Kalish Photo.

8

Preservers of History

BY JO ZSCHAU

Los Altos is indeed fortunate to have had so many of its early residents take an interest in chronicling the development of this area from wildflower-strewn fields to the carefully laid out downtown business triangle and nearby residential neighborhoods. Paul Shoup initiated the birth of the new community in 1907. In his manuscript, *The Birth of a Town*, Ed Woodworth described the first 25 years of its life, and Joe Salameda continued the history through the 1970s in his book, *Memories of Los Altos*.

In 1954 J. Gilbert Smith sold his apricot orchard to the newly-incorporated City of Los Altos for its planned Civic Center, and willed his Craftsman-style farm house and remaining acre of land to the city. In 1974 the City Council formed the Los Altos Historical Commission and voted to turn the Smith house into an historical museum. It opened to the public on December 1, 1977, the 25th anniversary of the City's incorporation.

The Los Altos History House Museum is both a repository of the area's memorabilia (historic photographs, bound volumes of early issues of the *Los Altos News* and *Los Altos Town Crier*, personal collections of Los Altos Hills historian, Florence Fava, and City officials Audrey Fisher and George Estill) and a house museum furnished in the style of a 1930s farm house.

Through the efforts of the Los Altos Historical Commission, the apricot orchard at the Civic Center has been designated a local historical landmark reflecting the area's agricultural heritage. The Commission was also responsible for having local historical designation plaques placed on the facades of several early Main Street buildings. When the old garage on the corner of First and State Streets was demolished, the Historical Commission recommended that the new buildings be similar in height and architectural detail to the original buildings on Main Street, thus perpetuating the same feeling of scale and rhythm. □

A sampling of historical materials available to the public at the Los Altos History House Museum. Photo by Christiane Dubrulle.

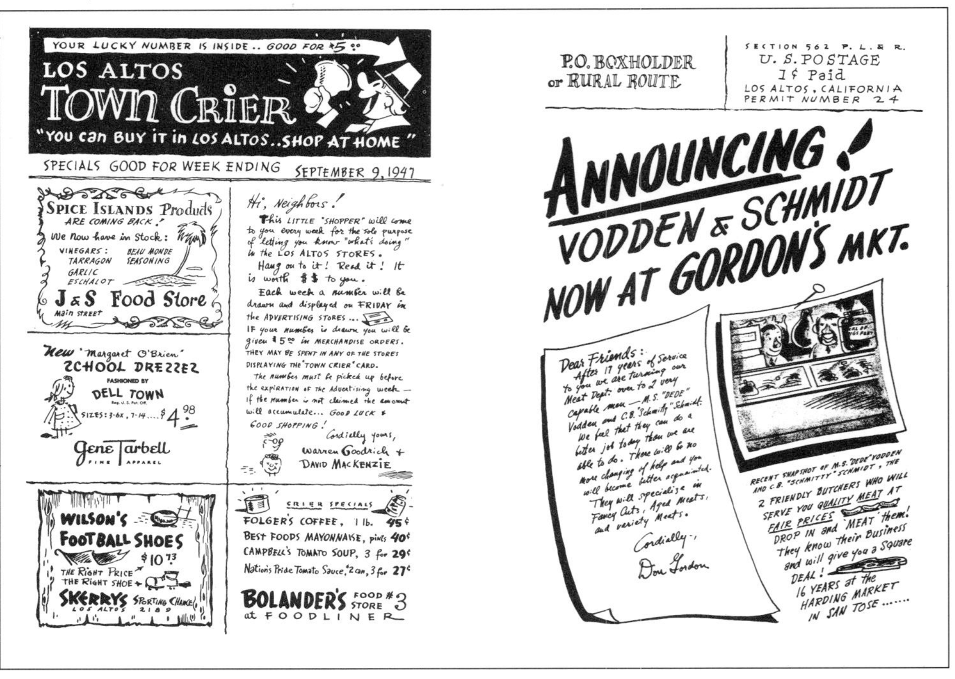

YOUR LUCKY NUMBER IS INSIDE.. GOOD FOR $5.00

LOS ALTOS TOWN CRIER

"YOU CAN BUY IT IN LOS ALTOS..SHOP AT HOME"

SPECIALS GOOD FOR WEEK ENDING SEPTEMBER 9, 1947

SPICE ISLANDS Products ARE COMING BACK!
We now have in Stock:
VINEGARS: TARRAGON, GARLIC, ESCHALOT
BEAU MONDE SEASONING
J & S Food Store
Main Street

Hi, Neighbors!
This little "shopper" will come to you every week for the sole purpose of letting you know "what's doing" in the Los Altos stores.
Hang on to it! Read it! It is worth $$ to you.
Each week a number will be drawn and displayed on FRIDAY in the ADVERTISING STORES ... IF your number is drawn you will be given $5.00 in MERCHANDISE ORDERS. THEY MAY BE SPENT IN ANY OF THE STORES DISPLAYING THE "TOWN CRIER" CARD.
The numbers must be picked up before the expiration of the Advertising week — if the number is not claimed the amount will accumulate... GOOD LUCK & GOOD SHOPPING!
Cordially yours,
Warren Goodrich + David MacKenzie

New "Margaret O'Brien" SCHOOL DRESSES
FASHIONED BY DELL TOWN
SIZES: 3-6X, 7-14.... $4.98
Gene Tarbell
FINE APPAREL

WILSON'S FOOTBALL SHOES
$10.73
THE RIGHT PRICE
THE RIGHT SHOE
SKERRY'S SPORTING CHANCE
LOS ALTOS 2189

CRIER SPECIALS
FOLGER'S COFFEE, 1 lb. 45¢
BEST FOODS MAYONNAISE, pints 40¢
CAMPBELL'S TOMATO SOUP, 3 for 29¢
Nation's Pride Tomato Sauce, #2 can, 3 for 27¢
BOLANDER'S FOOD STORE #3
at FOODLINER

P.O. BOXHOLDER
or RURAL ROUTE

SECTION 562 P. L. & R.
U. S. POSTAGE
1¢ Paid
LOS ALTOS, CALIFORNIA
PERMIT NUMBER 24

ANNOUNCING!
VODDEN & SCHMIDT
NOW AT GORDON'S MKT.

Dear Friends:
After 17 years of Service to you we are turning our Meat Dept. over to 2 very capable men — M.S. "DEDE" Vodden and C.B. "Schmitty" Schmidt.
We feel that they can do a better job today than we are able to do. There will be no more changing of help and you will become better acquainted.
They will specialize in Fancy Cuts, Aged Meats, and variety Meats.
Cordially,
Don Gordon

RECENT SNAPSHOT OF M.S. "DEDE" VODDEN AND C.B. "SCHMITTY" SCHMIDT, THE 2 FRIENDLY BUTCHERS WHO WILL SERVE YOU QUALITY MEAT AT FAIR PRICES
DROP IN and "MEAT" them! They know their Business and will give you a Square DEAL!
16 YEARS at the HARDING MARKET IN SAN JOSE......

The first issue of the Los Altos Town Crier; it was a single sheet fold-over shoppers guide founded in 1947 by David MacKenzie.

Above left: The J. Gilbert Smith house, built in 1905, is a fitting site for the Los Altos History House Museum. Photo by Christiane Dubrulle.

Above: Los History House Association members, Peggy Gordon (left) and Jane Ridgway, work diligently on the archives at the History House Museum. Growing collections include bound volumes of newspapers, booklets, oral histories, photo albums, memorabilia, period furniture and artifacts. Photo by Christiane Dubrulle.

Left: Former living room of the Smith home has been restored with period furniture. Photo by Christiane Dubrulle.

Below: As a result of the volunteer efforts of the Apricot Alliance, the Eschenbruecher house which had been built in 1908 near downtown Los Altos, was moved to 26379 Fremont Avenue in Los Altos Hills where it serves as that town's Heritage House. Photo by Christiane Dubrulle.

Above: Looking down Main Street from First Street, circa 1930. Photo: History House Museum Archives

Main Street at Second Street, 1941 World War II Los Altos Disaster Relief and Preparedness Parade. Note the pharmacy building. History House Museum photo.

Old Horace Hill Barn and silos in Pink Horse Ranch near Foothill College, have been declared "historic" and have been preserved when other farm buildings were replaced with homes in 1982. The silos (right) now serve as "his" and "hers" dressing rooms at the homeowners' swimming pool. Photos by Marjorie Kellogg-Van Rheeden.

Above: Main Street 1992. Thriving businesses occupy the original buildings that now bear local historical designation plaques. Photo by Christiane Dubrulle.

Main Street at Second Street: 1992 Pet Parade. An old building has a facelift while maintaining its architectural character. Photo by Christiane Dubrulle.

Above: 1970. Among the "preservers of history" are the aerial photography professionals like Pacific Aerials of Oakland who have been covering the Bay Area annually since 1937. This aerial shows the almost treeless parking plazas abuzz with shoppers; Foothill Expressway had replaced the railroad tracks; the San Antonio School (right center) had not yet met the wreckers's ball, and San Antonio Road was already beginning to show signs of becoming "real estate row." Photo courtesy of Pacific Aerial Surveys of Oakland, California.

9

A Community with Heart

BY ANNE CHAPPELL

Los Altans are as diverse and multi-cultural as residents of any Bay Area city. But unlike many towns in fast-paced Silicon Valley, where neighbors remain strangers and community service is left up to state and county agencies, Los Altans are willing to pitch in to make their city a better place in which to grow up, live and retire.

This thread of community spirit was evident long before citizens voted to incorporate Los Altos. In 1905, E.D. Carothers opened his home as a gathering place for area youth to read, sing, dance and hold social events. Adults soon joined in the fun and in 1907, the group gave itself a name, the Music and Literary Club, and adopted a constitution that directed members "to help whatever is good, oppose whatever is evil, to give service wherever it is needed...."

When the club outgrew the Carothers' home, members built a clubhouse on San Antonio Road in 1908 and changed the group's name to the San Antonio Club. A women's sewing section of the club made thousands of garments a year for local needy families, the American Red Cross, Salvation Army and poor patients at O'Connor Hospital in San Jose. The original club lasted through 1930, but the women's section flourished for many more decades.

Another group that impacted Los Altos in its early days was the Parent Teacher Association. In 1915, the PTA conducted a postcard campaign to publicize the virtues of the town of Los Altos. In the late 1940s, under the leadership of Ruth Sutton, PTA members held sewing bees, hosted turkey dinners and planned a house-to-house campaign to raise money to build Covington Pool.

The community pool effort drew support from other community groups, including the humorous Father's Frolics. Three dozen dads left their humility behind to write and perform in their own spoofs, portraying both male and female characters. The first show, "Under the Gaslight," was a hit in 1954 and the Frolics went on to produce many more comedies over the next 14 years.

One of the most publicized community causes was the campaign to build a youth center. The Los Altos Foundation took on the project in 1956 and raised $61,404 with help from the Rancho Roundup, Los Altos Youth Club benefit car washes, Hidden Villa Horseplay Fiesta, Federated Women's Club fashion shows and other events. Even celebrity Bing Crosby donated $10,000 to the project in 1959.

In the 1970s, children's clothing store owner Marion Jackston and Cranberry Scoop owner Hope Higbee were mesmerized by the Main Street Electrical Parade at Disneyland. They decided to try something similar in Los Altos and recruited support from Walter Singer, former Los Altos Stationers owner, and Jack Huston, former co-owner of Russell-Huston

Members of the San Antonio Club, the oldest club in Los Altos, gather in costume for the annual Topsy Turvey Ball to celebrate the second anniversary of the 1906 earthquake. Photo courtesy of Barbara McCarthy.

Above: Boy Scouts attend flag raising ceremony at the Old Oak Tree at Main and First Streets in March, 1949.

Below: The Los Altos Newcomers Club was founded in 1952 by Ida Rudikoff (second from left) for the purpose of assisting new residents to become oriented to the community and make friends. The annual Halloween Costume Party was held at Pink Horse Ranch.

Men's Clothing Store. The four founders made costumes and designed their own, brightly-lit floats. The first parade was a modest affair, lasting only about 15 minutes. By the 1980s and '90s, under the volunteer leadership of Bob Grimm, Ed Barnes and others, the parade grew into an event that lasts an hour-and-a-half and lures nearly 40,000 people who line Main and State Streets to enjoy seven bands and more than 75 entries.

Like the Festival of Lights Parade, Hidden Villa has also become a mainstay of community service and recreation. More than 15,000 Bay Area school children now visit the 1,600-acre farm and wilderness preserve annually.

Westwind Barn is also operated by a non-profit organization and runs entirely on volunteer support. The barn is home to the 4-H riding for the handicapped program and about five annual horse-related events, including the September Hoe-down.

Los Altos today is bursting with similar examples of selfless community volunteerism. The cities of Los Altos and Los Altos Hills each year honor about nine community volunteers for thousands of hours of charitable work while the Board of Realtors bestows its prestigious Community Service Award on one dedicated person each year. But many other

volunteers quietly go about their business, unrecognized, like the Sock Monkey Ladies who sew stuffed monkeys for hospitalized children or the Quilting Bee owners and volunteers who handcrafted quilts for homeless children each holiday season. Also deserving mention are the five couples who decided in the early 90s to hold a joint Christmas party for their friends, charge them entrance fees and then donate thousands of dollars of proceeds from their Los Altos Charity Ball to Community Services Agency (CSA) of Mountain View, Los Altos and Los Altos Hills.

CSA in turn allocates money to a host of services that provide free donated food, clothing, job training and hot meals to low-income and homeless people. The agency also arranges in-home care and rides for seniors and is involved in providing nutritional meals to more than 120 seniors a day.

Besides helping their own at home, Los Altans reach out to the far corners of the earth to make friends. The Los Altos Sister Cities Inc. was formed in 1985 to search for a sister city. Now a separate non-profit entity, LASCI has linked Los Altos with three foreign towns: Bendigo, Victoria, Australia in 1987; Syktyvkar, Russia in 1989, and ShiLin, Taipai, Taiwan, in the mid-90s. Several formal delegations have traveled back and forth between the sister cities.

Los Altos Community Foundation has been developing an endowment fund in the past decade to provide resources for special Los Altos charities and community projects. In 1998 the foundation moved into their own offices in the Community House located adjacent to Hillview Community Center.

Whether it's sewing clothes for the needy or sock monkeys for hospitalized children, Los Altans throughout history have given of themselves to help those less fortunate and improve their own surroundings. In the process, they have created one of the most desirable places to live in the entire San Francisco Bay Area. □

Top: In the early 1990s volunteers sewed quilts at the Quilting Bee in Los Altos. They handcrafted 1,700 quilts in a year and half for the needy children served by the Emergency Housing Consortium. Volunteer quilters from left to right: Sharron Carleton, Lucy Rahn (holding Carleton's granddaughter, Lucy Sarafina Muson), Nancy Herman, Joan Freitas, Lois Warburton, Jean Rhodes and former Quilting Bee owner, Diana Leone. Photo by Matthew E. Durham.

Middle: The Festival of Lights Parade in 1991. Photo by Marjorie Kellogg-Van Rheeden.

Bottom: Louise Spangler works with Tanya, the first work-exchange intern from Syktyvkar, Russia, hosted by Los Altos Sister Cities.Photo by Matthew E. Durham.

Top: Two dads, Henry Humphry and Orville Landi, perform in the Fathers' Frolics production of "The Half Caste" to raise money for local causes.

Above: Sammy Kahn drives Alex Reikes (dressed as a woman) in Fathers' Frolics production of "The Half Caste" in February 1955.

Left: Program guide for the Fathers' Frolics as it appeared in the Shoppers' Guide in 1955.

Above: Former Mayor, Marge Bruno, a member of the first Los Altos delegation to Syktyvkar, is greeted by Russian hosts in native costume.

Left: (left to right) Art Carmichael Jr., Ray Skitt, Mary Prochnow, Pat Koening, Tom Kenna, Marion Grimm, Hazel Gibson, Nancy Wilde and Ann Bjorkland as they are being honored as the top community volunteers for Los Altos and Los Altos Hills in 1991.

Right: Volunteer merchants Conrad Heintzelman, Pinky Whelan and Sue Heesacker tie yellow ribbons to lampposts downtown in support of troops in the Middle East during the Persian Gulf War in 1991. Photo by Matthew E. Durham.

Above left: Six year old "John Wayne" shoots baskets from horseback as a method of improving balance and coordination skills. Photo by Matthew E. Durham.

Above: A happy, though needy, family leaves with their bag of Christmas gifts from Community Services Agency's Santa Claus exchange. Individual Los Altans, merchants and service clubs donate toys and food to CSA throughout the year. Photo by Charles Halleck.

Left: Sock hoppers at Rancho Shopping Center's Rock Back The Clock. The annual event raises money for the Los Altos Festival of Lights parade. Photo by Matthew E. Durham.

Below: Kristy Poindexter, 13, hugs sock monkeys handcrafted by a group of Los Altos seniors, known as the Sock Monkey Ladies. Photo by Matthew E. Durham.

10

The Arts Come to Town

BY DOYNE MRAZ

Arts usually spawn in large urban areas. Because Los Altos has been largely a rural area, the arts have not been influential in its development, but have served as a necessary codicil to the civilizing influences of the area. The first recorded "art" event was a theatrical production, called *The Matrimonial Advertisement*, in the San Antonio Club on April 4, 1908. No records of the success of the production remain. Apparently, the club house was used occasionally for other productions. In the early 1920s important families of Los Altos presented an "elaborate musicale" entitled *Farewell to Pan* in an open-air pavilion called the Ng Tong Temple. In the 30s, it was noted that people from Los Altos had to travel to Palo Alto to pay 20 cents to see a movie.

During the 1940s, however, the need for a motion picture theater was realized. In August, 1948, a construction trailer was moved to the theater site on Main Street. Hal Honore, overseeing the "Peninsula Theatre Fraternity" threw open the doors for a grand opening on May 18, 1949, with Davis Peterson as manager. The long awaited facility was open; admission was 74 cents for adults and loge seats were 90 cents. The theater possessed the ultimate in screen and projection equipment, and the *Los Altos Times* advertised the occasion as a "new high in entertainment."

Most recently, the arts have grown rapidly in Los Altos. In 1965, the Los Altos Youth Theater was established by actress Vivian Vance's sister, Lou Ann Hall. That same year, Foothill College built a theater, which still presents professional quality theater. In 1975, Music for Minors was born and, through the leadership of Grace Johnston, the group has taught music in the schools on the Mid-Peninsula. In 1976, the Los Altos Conservatory Theater was established by Doyne Mraz, Professor of Theater at Foothill College. L'ACT was replaced by a new stage company in the mid-90s, the Bus Barn Stage Company.

July, 1952: Director Harold Brady puts his chorus line of lovelies through a fast rehearsal for the "Foothill Follies"—first presentation by a new group called the Los Altos Foothill Players. Early shows were held in the old Pink Horse Ranch barn. Reprinted from the Town Crier.

One of the most important contributions to the arts was the establishment of the city's Arts Committee, which yearly holds a contest for "art in public places." Los Altos enjoys numerous sculptures in public parks, and public-minded citizens have purchased several of the pieces for permanent display. □

Above: Ng Tong Temple, 1937. View from May Ansley's backyard, now Shoup Park. Five families who owned adjacent properties built the temple for theatrical productions. Included were the families of Guy Shoup, Albert Robinson, Charles "Cheerio" Field, Frank Oliver and Robert Newton Lynch. History House Museum photo.

Above: Los Altos settlers, costumed for a play, pose in front of the Guy Shoup home. Standing: Lida Coliver, Estelle Oliver, Mrs. Sheaf, Harriet Ames and Faith Shoup Robinson. Seated: M. Shoup, Charles Field and Rose Shoup. History House Museum photo.

Below: Los Altos motion picture. Part of the cast looking over the script at the home of Frank Oliver. The film, called Rebecca, *was written by Guy Shoup. (left to right) Mr. Berry, owner of Los Altos Livery stable, Faith Shoup Robinson, Charles Field and Burton Noble. History House Museum photo.*

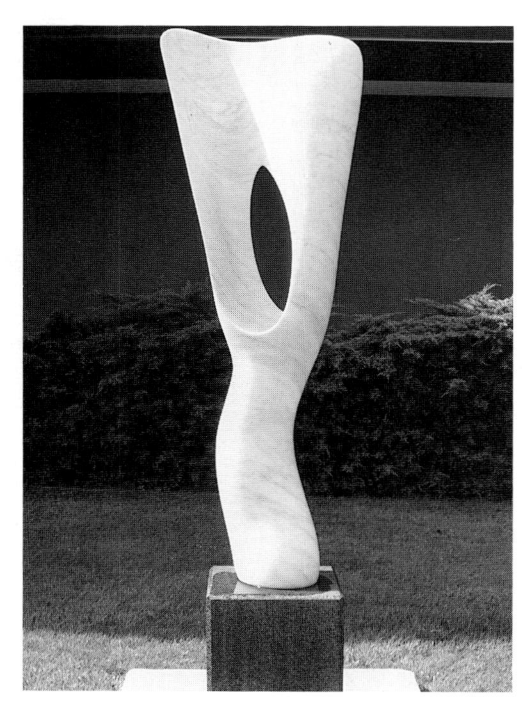

Sculptures in Los Altos: Right: Sculpture by T. Barney at Los Altos Sequoia Fire Station, 1992.

Far right: Sculpture at Foothill College Library

Bottom: Famed Bay Area Sculptor Benny Bufano's "Bear" is focus of attention at Bullis School in Los Altos Hills. All photos on page by Marjorie Kellogg Van-Rheeden.

Above: Los Altos moving picture theater with its Art Deco exterior. Taken in 1951. The theatre closed in 1976. History House Museum photo.

Left: Home to Los Altos Conservatory Theatre (L'ACT), since 1976, this converted service building on civic center grounds, provides an intimate setting for the 14 professional plays provided to Los Altans annually. Photo by Christiane Dubrulle.

Below: Part of the cast during a 1992 performance of "Bleacher Bums" by Joe Mantegna at LACT. Photo by Ginger Bate.

11

The Library: An Enduring Resource

BY CAROL TEFFT

Los Altos was a sleepy village in July of 1914, but the residents did love to read and something important was about to happen. C.E. Minor, a Los Altos land agent, made the county a proposal it couldn't turn down: for $5 a month, he would open and run a library with 50 books in his land office at First and Main Streets. Thus on July 25 was born the first branch of the county library. In the next few years the library was housed in various buildings including the Copeland Building, Shoup Building and the Scout Hall. The books had increased to 500 and the paycheck to $10 a month in 1921 when Jessie Landels became the Los Altos Librarian. Jessie and later her husband, Rev. Thomas Landels, were the librarians until 1944.

In 1934, the Southern Pacific Power House, an ivy covered building on First Street, had been vacant for several years. Paul and Guy Shoup led a group of Los Altans who provided paint and materials, the W.P.A. furnished the labor, and together they transformed the old power house into a library, leased from S.P. for $1 a year until 1957.

In 1956 a group of girl scouts asked the mayor to study library needs. As a result of the Mayor's Committee recommendation, the Friends of the Library formed and voters passed the first of four successful library measures. In 1960 the Civic Center Library was built and in 1975 bonds for Woodland Library in south Los Altos were passed. In 1985 a 5-year tax for extended hours passed, and in 1990 the public voted by 74% to extend the tax and double the size of the Civic Center Library. The citizens of Los Altos and Los Altos Hills obviously still love to read, as did those in 1914, and they still vigorously support their libraries. □

From 1934 to 1957, the old power house on First Street served the community as the library.

Top: The first bond measure ever passed in Los Altos made possible the building of the library at the Civic Center. The 10,000 sq. ft. building was built for under $200,000 in 1963.

Above left: Girl Scout Troop 40 made history in 1956 when members took the library as their community project and asked the Mayor to study library service needs. Jill Sweeten (left) and Barbara Moor of Troop 40.

Above right: Friends of the Library formed in 1957 and began to raise money for the library through book sales. From left to right: Mrs. James Nall, Mrs. Guy Gugliotta and Mrs. Robert Noyce.

Left: In 1991, it was time to build again. Assemblyman Charles Quackenbush (22nd District) spoke at the ground breaking for the new addition to the Los Altos Community Library. Seated, left to right: Los Altos Hills Mayor Sid Hubbard, County Supervisor Dianne McKenna and Los Altos Mayor, Denny Spangler.

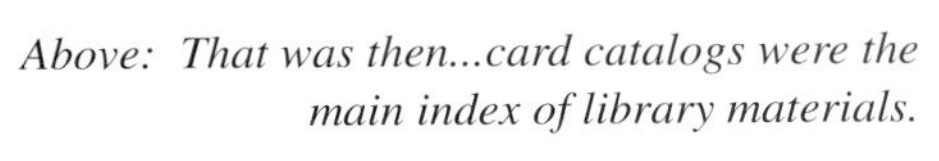

Above: That was then...card catalogs were the main index of library materials.

Right: This is now...computers furnish greater access to library materials and make research faster and more efficient.

Below: Construction begins in 1992 for the library expansion. Photo by Christiane Dubrulle.

Below right: Exhibiting local pride at the 1992 construction site are Los Altos residents, left to right: Paul Jenkinson, Project Manager; Judy Dahl, Library Commission Chair; Carol Tefft, Head librarian, and Robert Cavigli, President of Ehrlich Rominger, the architectural firm that designed the new addition.

Above: Another successful bond measure made possible the construction of the Woodland Library in south Los Altos in 1975 as well as an additional 4,000 square feet at the Civic Center Library.

Left: Children's Story Time remains one of the most popular events at the Los Altos Library. One of the Children's Librarians, Sharon Kelly, shares stories with Los Altos children. Photo courtesy of Town Crier.

12

SPIRITUAL DIMENSIONS

BY DON GRANT

The spiritual roots of Los Altos may date back to the days of the early missionaries such as Father Junipero Serra. The documented activity is a bit more recent. In 1908 Rev. Oliver Hister was appointed pastor of a Methodist church which met in the Shoup Building. In 1913, the Methodist church ceased to exist, returning as the United Methodist Church in 1950.

In 1914, a small group of Episcopalians constructed the first church building, now Foothills Congregational Church, on Orange Avenue. In the same year, the Union Church on San Antonio Road was built under the leadership of Rev. George W. Hunter, formerly the Protestant chaplain at San Quentin. The congregation later became the Union Presbyterian on University Avenue. Around 1927 Father Stack established the Jesuit Retreat House for laymen. It wasn't until 1942 that the first Catholic Church, St. Nicholas, was built.

In 1940, Mr. & Mrs. Rupert Peterson established a Baptist ministry that grew into First Baptist of Los Altos, chartered in 1945. In 1947, at 140 Main Street the First Baptist Church buildings were started. This building is now the Masonic Lodge. In 1967, the current site on Magdalena was established. Also that year, Congregation Beth Am began construction on its current facility on Arastradero Road under the leadership of Rabbi Sidney Akselrad.

Los Altos has a unique spiritual community. Ministers tend to stay in local churches longer than the average length of stay for a particular denomination. Although each denomination started out to meet the needs of its own congregation, the community spirit of Los Altos soon brought congregations together to meet the needs of the community.

Two events in the 1980s caused local churches to unite for a common cause. First, the 1989 earthquake. Fifteen seconds of nature's power caused Los Altos congregations to respond to the needs of hard hit areas such as Watsonville and Santa Cruz. Second was the reality of the homeless problem in Los Altos. The combined efforts of the Los Altos churches formed the Alpha Omega Rotating Shelter Program. This program has become a role model for other communities. Los Altos can be proud of its spiritual dimensions, both past and present. □

Top: Union Church on San Antonio Road at Whitney Street built 1914-15. History House Museum Photo.

Bottom: Christ Episcopal Church 1914 on Orange Avenue. History House Museum photo.

Opposite page: 1950 aerial of El Retiro Retreat Center in foreground, St. Nicholas Church near top of photo. Note water tower on University Avenue. Photo by Hatfield Aerial Survey. Courtesy of El Retiro Retreat.

Top: Architects' model of Congregation Beth Am of Los Altos Hills before construction began. Photo courtesy of Congreation Beth Am.

Right: Ground breaking ceremony in 1967 of Congregation Beth Am; Rabbi Sidney Akselrad is holding the shovel. Photo by Sheldon Block

Below: Churches of Los Altos unite to aid 1989 earthquake victims. In picture: Don Grant and Jeff Nash of Foothill Baptist Church load supplies for Watsonville. Photo by Jenna Calk.

Below: With a vision for a new church, Pastor Ralph Craft (third from left) and church leaders study the site of the First Baptist Church on Magdalena formerly part of the Hale Ranch. On the right below is aerial view of First Baptist Church as it looked in 1992. Photos courtesy of First Baptist Church.

Top: Outdoor service before building at United Methodist Church of Los Altos in 1950, Rev. Cox presiding. Photo by Philip Becke.

Left: United Methodist Church of Los Altos in 1992. Courtesy of United Methodist Church.

Below left: Los Altos/Mountain View Ministers Association retreat, 1992. Photo by Don Grant.

Below right: Foothills Congregational Church create "Mayflower" float for Festival of Lights Parade. Photo by Marjorie Kellogg-Van Rheeden.

13

Pioneers From Everywhere

BY HONOR SPITZ

Perhaps no place on earth has more diversity of culture, landscape, topography and history than the Bay Area, and the town of Los Altos is no exception. Behind and beyond the "quaint village atmosphere" moniker so often ascribed to this bedroom community on the mid-Peninsula, lie the stories of forefathers that go back hundreds of years. Whereas some countries have castles and fortressed communities as physical evidence of their long and illustrious past, our heritage is to be found in the generous abundance of everything that one sees today. Where else is one likely to see, in the same area, the architecture of the Mediterranean, the Japanese, the Italians or the English, or to be able to walk down a city street and sample the foods of half a dozen or more ethnic groups? The names and faces of these many different peoples make up our proud heritage.

Paul Shoup

When the Spanish explorers first came to California, they encountered Indians who had been at home here for hundreds of years. And as so many "explorers" since then, the Spanish were so taken by the beauty and potential of the land that they decided that they had reached their journey's end. Not only that, they secured large portions of real estate commonly referred to as "Spanish Land Grants", vast ranches snatched from the Indians and granted to the "Dons" who followed in the wake of the Spanish missionaries. Eventually, the Dons sold out to the first wave of European settlers, who in turn employed not only others from that continent, but Chinese and later Japanese. The latter two were not permitted to be landowners for many generations. Slovenians, Portuguese, Italian, Swiss, German and Irish all found their way to "The Valley of Hearts Delight" for a variety of reasons, and many of them settled here.

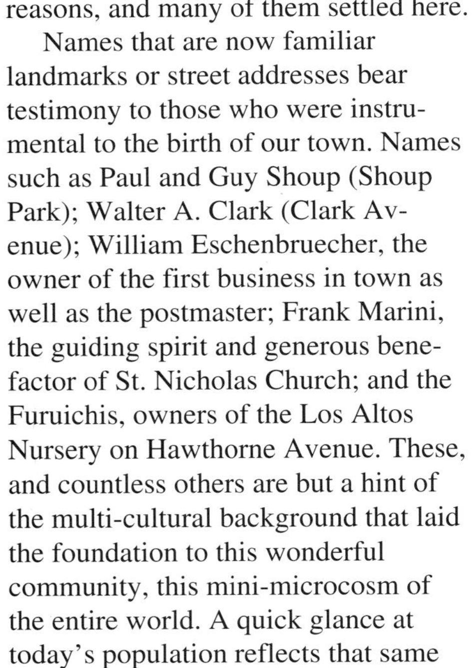

Names that are now familiar landmarks or street addresses bear testimony to those who were instrumental to the birth of our town. Names such as Paul and Guy Shoup (Shoup Park); Walter A. Clark (Clark Avenue); William Eschenbruecher, the owner of the first business in town as well as the postmaster; Frank Marini, the guiding spirit and generous benefactor of St. Nicholas Church; and the Furuichis, owners of the Los Altos Nursery on Hawthorne Avenue. These, and countless others are but a hint of the multi-cultural background that laid the foundation to this wonderful community, this mini-microcosm of the entire world. A quick glance at today's population reflects that same spirit of generosity, that feeling that all are welcome and that there is room for people of all nationalities. □

Paul Shoup home on University Avenue. Built 1906-1910. History House Museum photo.

Eschenbruecher house, 130 Second Street. Built in 1908. First home in downtown Los Altos by first merchant and postmaster. History House Museum.

Billy Eschenbruecher
First Postmaster and merchant
History House Museum photo

Marini House at 220 University. Picture taken May 1978. History House Museum photo.

Frank Marini
1862-1952
History House Museum photo

Top: 1952, owners and employees at Los Altos Nursery gathered for this photo. Front row: Frank Furuichi, Herb Tamada, Tom Furuichi, George Furuichi, Sally (last name unknown) and Agapita Rubacalva; back row: Tad Tani, Tosh Tasbakimoto, Ben Furuichi, Helen Furuichi Miyake and Yachi Miyake. Frank Furuichi Sr. purchased five acres on Hawthorne Avenue in 1918. The Los Altos Nursery is still serving Los Altans on the same site. Photo courtesy of Los Altos Nursery.

Center: Mabel Eschenbruecher was married to Roy, the son of Billy Eschenbruecher who owned and operated the first downtown business. History House Museum photo.

Bottom: A Japanese School functioned in 1920s in Los Altos. History House Museum photo.

Opposite page: pioneer humanitarians Josephine and Frank Duveneck of Hidden Villa, photo by Carolyn Caddes, 1977.

14

Recreation For All

BY WULF SCHRADER

San Francisco 49er quarterback, former and current Olympic athletes, iron-man competitors, triathletes, ranked equestrians, nationally ranked tennis players and golfers are just a few of the many sportsmen and women who have made Los Altos their home and have raised families here. Going back to the turn of the century, bike riding was a popular craze in America and Los Altos was no exception. It was a practical way of getting about. Swimming, horseback riding, fishing and hunting were primary recreational activities.

With the advent of the interurban electric railroad in the spring of 1910, Los Altos became a stop-off point for people seeking recreation through the Santa Clara Valley. For many San Franciscans, the Santa Cruz beaches were regarded as their summer playground, and Los Altos was a pleasant halfway point. Picturesque Adobe Creek that ran through the town became an anglers haven and trout were taken from the creek well into the 1960s. Plans were underway in 1919 for a frontier log cabin style building for the original Boy Scout troop in Los Altos, including an auditorium and a swimming pool along the creek. This was never built, but Los Altans have always been well aware of the need for recreation.

A long rectangular, boxy, shingled building known as the Scout Hall was built in 1922 on First Street near the livery stable and marked the first site of an indoor basketball court in Los Altos. A multipurpose structure, it served for four decades as a community meeting place for groups like the Boy and Girl Scouts and for socials and dances, definitely a step up from holding dances in the livery stable.

Outside athletic activities took place in the fields directly to the south of the hall. Prior to this, similar activities took place in the Shoup Building on Main Street and in the area outside the Los Altos Grammar School, which was completed in 1911 and enlarged in 1922 to include an auditorium in the rear of the building. The grammar school's baseball team in 1917 traveled to neighboring towns to play their games.

May Day and the Fourth of July celebrations in Los Altos provided the earliest use of recreational facilities, and family picnics and gatherings took place on a regular basis. Today that tradition is carried on in a civic celebration at Shoup Park on the Fourth of July.

In the late 20s and early 30s, Frank and Josephine Duveneck purchased most of the land that became Hidden Villa. The first American Youth Hostel west of the Mississippi was established there and housed many young foreign visitors. The Duvenecks gave their ranch to Santa Clara County and now

Second Section

San Jose Mercury Her

SAN JOSE, CALIFORNI : THURSDAY MORNING, APRIL 17

)S ALTOS BOY SCOUTS WILL BE THE ENVY OF ALL OTHER ROOPS WHEN THEY HAVE THEIR PROPOSED NEW CLUB HOME

il Shoup, Charles K. Field, nd Other San Francisco Men on Committee.

lding Will Be Erected in City Park on Bank of Picturesque Stream.

By STAFF REPORTER.

OS ALTOS, April 16.—The Boy Scouts of Los Altos will soon be regarded with envy by the boys of other scout organizations over the state, for the boys are to have a home of their own, devoted exclusively to their uses, built for them and owned by them.

Plans now under consideration, which will, undoubtedly, be carried through, provide for a permanent home for the Boy Scouts organization in the city park, on the bank of the Los Altos creek. The building will be of natural logs on the exterior, copying the appearance of the frontier log cabin of the early days of California.

The interior of the building will be divided into an auditorium, library and general club room, and in addition to this a swimmnig pool for the boys will be constructed on the creek.

In addition to providing a place where the boys of the organization can hold their official gatherings, the new home will give them a club where they can hold other meetings, either for games and entertainment, and, in fact, the proposed

MEMBERS OF BOY SCOUTS TROOP OF LOS ALTOS WHO ARE TO HAVE FINE CLUB BUILDING.—Engravement by Melvin, Roberts & Horwarth.

such men as Paul Schoup, director of the Southern Pacific; Charles K. Field, editor of Sunset Magazine; Captain H. Melsom, and other business and professional men of San Francisco who make their homes in Los Altos.

At a meeting held recently in the

solute faith in the purposes of this committee and many of the members of the committee have sons who are members of the Bo yScouts organization. Another meeting of the committee is to be held within a short time, and at that meeting the plans will very likely, it is under-

Scouts of Los Altos have actively participated in war work activities and several war medals awarded them for faithful work. The will be used in the coming Victory loan drive to help in putting Los Altos district "over the top."

125,922 PEOPLE IN CARE OF THE STATE

Statistics Given at Meeting of Rotary Club at Hotel Montgomery Yesterday.

Election of San Jose Man as District Governor Cheered by Local Club.

Startling statistics on the number of people wholly or partly in the care of the state were given by the Rev. Father Charles A. Ramm, pastor of St. Mary's cathedral in San Francisco at the luncheon meeting of the Rotary club at Hotel Montgomery yesterday. Father Ramm is a member of the state board of charities and corrections and was representing the board officially.

He showed that there are in 14 state institutions such as prisons, asylums and homes for the feebleminded, an annual population of more than 82,000, with 125,922 as the total number of people the state either cares for directly or through their houses, hospitals, orphanages, orphans' aids and in private families approved by state agencies. He touched on the terrific cost of this service and of the causes which underlie these conditions and the remedies which are offered.

Convention Report.

Arthur F. Holmes, one of the delegates to the recent conference in San Diego, reported on the convention and the wonderful reception which the delegates received not only in San Diego but in the cities en route as well.

Louis Campiglia announced that

Farmers' Central

Te Farmers' oldest and la tutions in Sa opened a bra Market. for th many resident of the city w cation more of the main Clara street. branch occupi A large stoc ral provision all times, an been provided utensils and

Top: Los Altos Boy Scout club house launching makes headlines in the San Jose Mercury News, 1915.

Above: Outings to Yosemite were not unusual in the 1920s. Here are Los Altans Robert Bleibler and his wife Violet at Yosemite.

Above: 1915 High flyers enjoy recess on playground equipment at Los Altos Grammar School. During the period 1910-1920 there were more children than adults in Los Altos

Left: May pole at Hidden Villa, 1992. Photo by Marjorie Kellogg-Van Rheeden.

Hidden Villa provides, in addition to the hostel, outdoor activities for thousands of children, as well as miles of wilderness hiking trails.

In the 1940s and 50s, the well-known Pink Horse Ranch bustled with recreational activities for families from miles around with lakeside activities, swimming and trout pond.

By the time the city of Los Altos was incorporated in 1952 every city block had at least one home with a swimming pool and plans were on the drawing board for establishing a first-rate high school which was eventually built in 1956.

In the 1960s, if you were looking for a recreational playground you needed to look only as far as the nearby foothills as the newly constructed Foothill Junior College provided an Olympic-sized pool, and a full range of athletic programs, including a strong, nationally-competitive tennis program.

In 1970, Los Altos High School's track and field team won the state championship, a feat never again achieved by a Los Altos athletic team in a public or private institution.

In the 1980s, the majority of Los Altos' dozen public parks were in place thanks to a strong parks and recreation department within the city and a city council that understood the needs of the community for accessible open areas for recreation that would appeal to all ages. For several years a New Year's Day "Fun Run," was sponsored by the city's recreation department for runners and joggers. Los Altos also provides traditional organized sports like Little League and Pony League baseball, AYSO soccer, YMCA basketball, Covington Critters Swim Club, Master's Swim Club and an annual Junior Olympics. □

Top: 1992. Olde Town Band entertains at a Sunday concert in Shoup Park. Photo by Wulf Schrader.

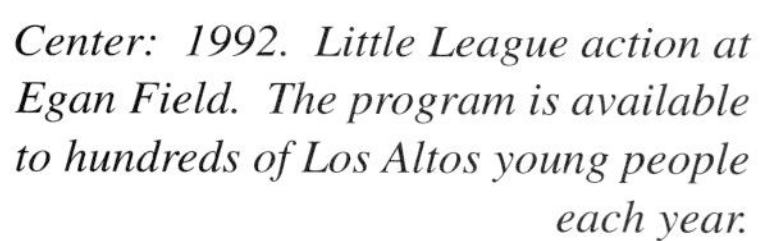

Center: 1992. Little League action at Egan Field. The program is available to hundreds of Los Altos young people each year.

Bottom: 1917. Los Altos Grammar School baseball team. Photo courtesy of Buswell Family Collection.

Top: 1959. Orchards and ranches created a country atmosphere. Here is the Engman Farm located at what is today Natoma and Black Mountain Roads. Photo courtesy of Marjorie Kellogg-Van Rheeden.

Center: circa 1964. Overflow crowd attends one of many competitions in Foothill College's Olympic-sized pool. Note the media coverage!

Bottom: Cyclists share the roadway with automobiles in 1992--just as they shared the highways with horses and buggies a century earlier. Photo by Wulf Schrader.

PINK HORSE RANCH.
Los Altans have always known how to have a good time. This classic overview of the Pink Horse Ranch was taken May 27, 1951–a Memorial Day weekend extravanganza. Count the cars and then try to find the hundreds of people who came with them!

Moody Road, the old Pescadero Stage Road, leads on to the Adobe Lodge, which flourished for a number of years as a recreation haven, and then to Hidden Villa, still a very active place for fun in the 1990s.

Photo provided by Los Altos Hills Historian, Rosemary Meyerott.

15

Community Scrapbook

EDITOR'S CHOICE

Rock Back The Clock 1990. Dressed as 50s rock star, James Dean, is seven-year-old Aaron Kaye. Photo by Matthew E. Durham.

Sepideh Moafi, 6, of Mountain View (left) and Lauren Batchelder, 9, of Los Altos, share a silly moment after classes at Almond Elementary School. Photo by Melissa Marciano.

Top, left: Four generations of a family, all of whom have lived in Los Altos continuously all of their lives (except Harry Buswell who moved here in 1906 when he was two years old). Left to right: John Schrader, Kathleen Frederick Schrader, Joyce Buswell Frederick, Harry Buswell. 1992 photo by Christiane Dubrulle.

Top, right: 1962. Year of the big snow in Los Altos. Photo Courtesy of Town Crier.

Center, right: July, 1987. Flash fire strikes Los Altos Hills homes along Arastradero and Page Mill Roads destroying 10 expensive homes. Photo by Marjorie Kellogg-Van Rheeden.

Right: Ranch of billionaire, the late David Packard in Los Altos Hills overlooks the San Francisco Bay. 1992 photo by Marjorie Kellogg-Van Rheeden.

Above: Raphael Meyers, a student at a military academy in Palo Alto, proudly shows off the car his mother gave him on his 14th birthday. He grew up in the large home at the intersection of Almond Avenue and San Antonio Road in Los Altos. His father, a San Francisco physician, in 1912 decided that San Francisco was "no place to raise a family" and so moved "to the country" in Los Altos. The home has been restored and is visible from San Antonio Road. History House Museum photo.

Right: Walter Singer, fondly known as Mr. Los Altos at one of his last public appearances before his death in 1992. He served as Honorary Chair of the "Spirit of The Hills" celebration in 1991. Photo by Marjorie Kellogg-Van Rheeden.

Below: Outline shows property purchased from long time resident, John Lohman, for the Foothill College campus. Lower right is Moody Road, which extends toward downtown as El Monte. Interstate 280 would later cross the approximate center of the picture from left to right. 1948 photo courtesy of John Lohman.

Above: 1972 Miss Los Altos Contestants. Photo courtesy of Ginny Lear, Los Altos Chamber of Commerce.

Upper right: Gardner Bullis used a wicker basket for his brief case. He was the first city attorney at no fee. Photo by Marjorie Kellogg-Van Rheeden.

Center right: "Artificial flowers" were popular during 1987-1992 drought years.

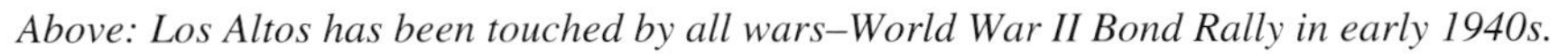

Above: Los Altos has been touched by all wars–World War II Bond Rally in early 1940s.

Right: Symbol of Los Altos concern during 1991 Operation Desert Storm was Jill Nyberg Peterson, who as a member of a National Guard Engineer group was among the first American military women in history to be sent into ground combat missions in Iraq.

Above: Hayfield at "Feather Hill Farm" on Old Trace Lane in Los Altos Hills was landing field for Ruolf Isenberg's plane. Circles were plowed in field to mark landing strip. Property later owned by John (LAH Mayor) and Eleanor Cranston Fowle. Photo provided by Marjorie Kellogg-Van Rheeden.

Right: The Hermann Bleibler family of Los Altos on an outing in their 1908 air-cooled Franklin. Mr. Bleibler was a well known blacksmith and wagon maker who created much of the ornate wrought-iron work that graces numerous historic buildings in the area. Photo courtesy of Marjorie and Armond King.

Goodbye . . .
Photo by Melissa A. Marciano.

16

THE LAST DECADE

BY BRUCE BARTON

Los Altos, the bedroom community where nothing ever happens, some residents are proud to boast, experienced changes aplenty in the 1990s. Not that it could be helped, really. Los Altos was not unlike any Silicon Valley community reflecting the boom of high-tech progress and prosperity. Cell phones were everywhere, as were the proliferation of SUVs and other large family vehicles that relegated little economy cars to the age of the dinosaurs.

The emergence of the Internet and its seemingly endless possibilities went over well in Los Altos. The Town Crier was one of first weekly papers in the nation to go online and offer an internet site representing the entire community.

Downtown, for better or worse, reflected the increasing commercialism and chain-store domination of the '90s. The arrival of Starbucks at the intersection of Main and Second Street, for instance, marked an even bigger event than the high-profile reconstruction and repaving of Main and State streets in 1993 and 1995, respectively.

A large crowd gathered to cheer the opening of a large addition to the Los Altos Main Library on April 18, 1993. Additional space was provided for the children's area, a program room and library materials.

Starbucks became an immediate attraction for hip java drinkers, cell phone in one hand, coffee in the other, the Wall Street Journal close by. It was definitely a place to meet, to engage in the neighborliness that has traditionally marked Los Altos. On the other hand, it signified a deterioration of the "village atmosphere," a downtown that had been filled with mom-and-pop operations, where visitors reveled in the low-key environment.

The new community plaza was among several eye-catching additions to the Los Altos landscape during the 1990s. Out was the old McElroy lumber yard at Foothill Expressway and San Antonio Road. In was the Gateway Building. Out was the old Rancho Market at Rancho Shopping Center. In was Andronico's and a renovated shopping center.

A permanent new home for the 50-year-old Los Altos Town Crier became a village landmark on Main Street in 1995 styled after early American architecture.

Realtors were having a field day in the 1990s as the median home prices in Los Altos and Los Altos Hills rose dramatically. The average home sale price in Los Altos went from about $550,000 in 1990 to the $1 million range in 1999.

Demographically, Los Altos was also changing. For many years best known for its large population of longtime, older residents, the 1990s saw a large increase in the number of young families - successful thirty- and forty-something executives with preschoolers and primary school-age kids looking for a safe bedroom community to call home. A 1997 survey showed the average Los Altos age at 42.4 years.

The Community House at 183 Hillview Avenue was established in 1998 by the Los Altos Community Foundation as a service for local non-profit organizations.

Los Altos fit the bill perfectly with its quiet, rural and safe residential streets. The success of Silicon Valley and its new wealth brought in people who could afford the skyrocketing housing costs of Los Altos and Los Altos Hills. Those who could buy Los Altos properties wanted to make the best of them. Bigger, more elaborate housing was the order of the latter half of the decade, and such desires weren't always consistent with residents in their 1950s era ranch style homes. City officials tried in vain to handle a housing design problem that one city councilmember described as trying to apply objectivity to subjectivity.

Local schools felt the impact of this new growth. The Los Altos School District grew by more than 600 students in the 1990s and was expected to peak at more than 3,700 by 2001. The growth brought calls from both the elementary school district and the high school district for bond measures to fund needed expansion and upgrading of the deteriorating school facilities. Voters passed both measures, a $58 million bond for the high schools in 1995 and a $94.7 million bond for the elementary schools in 1998. By the end of the century construction was midstream on the high school and plans finalized for the upgrades to the elementary schools.

Chef Lawrence Chu was selected the first annual Los Altan Of The Year by the Los Altos Town Crier in 1995.

This rise in a young Los Altos population meant greater city attention to parks. Los Altos bought 5.5 acres of land in the middle of town that came to be known as the Rosita Park. As the decade came to a close, soccer and baseball fields were being readied for the site and talks of a large recreational facility continued.

Traffic--and what to do about it--also dominated discussion in the 1990s as Los Altos vehicles flooded downtown streets and major arteries in and out of town. Lunchtime parking on some Fridays downtown was a near impossibility. But the parking question met with far more debate and discussion than action.

The decade also saw the deaths of some world-renowned icons who called this corner of the earth their home. Legendary author, Wallace Stegner, a longtime friend to environmental causes, died in 1993 after a car accident. David Packard, who along with Bill Hewlett formed one of the most successful companies in the world, died in 1996. The death of Packard, one of the fathers of Silicon Valley and a giant among philanthropic figures, triggered the expansion of the Los Altos-based Packard Foundation, with assets skyrocketing past the $10 billion mark. The foundation, with its broad range of programs and grants, became one the nation's biggest foundations virtually overnight.

Los Altos began the 21st century addressing the same kinds of challenges the communities faced in the 1990s - population growth, traffic, parking, affordable housing and the encroachment of new technologies. But, as the intimate residential streets show, the Los Altos' small-town environment is well established, and it continually draws people who want to add to - and not detract from - that neighborly atmosphere. □

At century's end, a $2.6 million Education Center was under construction adjacent to the History House Museum.

Photos courtesy of Los Altos Town Crier.

In March 1994, a Fifty-Year Time Capsule was installed in the new Community Plaza at Main and State streets.

Local artist R.J. Truman created a larger than life sculpture, "Cradle of Liberty," as a veteran's memorial in Shoup Park.

After 25 years as an unsightly empty lot, Conner Park was completed and dedicated in October 1999, as was Rosita Park near the Covington School.

The Parc Regent retirement community became a reality on property across from Los Altos City Hall at Edith Avenue and San Antonio Road.

Day workers congregating near the intersection of San Antonio and El Camino Real created a 10-year controversy that was addressed in late 1999 when the city drafted a no-solicitation ordinance.

Residents take advantage of Internet access on the many computers at the public library that unlocked the mysteries of the world wide web.

After almost a year of controversy, gas-powered blowers were declared illegal in Los Altos.

A community paint-by-the-numbers mural was completed by more than 100 children and adults to close out the century. Drafted by artist Jim M'Guinness, the mural depicts 100 years of life in Los Altos.

SPONSORS

Following is a list of those who ordered this book prior to publication to benefit Los Altos Tomorrow.

Martha & Bill Abbey
Ted & Margaret Abe
Keith, Kraig, Kirk, Kris Abe
Adventure Toys/Teacher Supplies
Abigail Lynn Ahrens
Alpine Image Systems, Inc.
Alto Associates, Inc
Marge & Roger Anderson
The Steve Anderson Family
Jonathan & Bridget Angin
The Angin Family
Dushan Angius
The Frederick L. Butterworth Family
Back Door Sandwich Shop
The Backs Family
Bank of the West
Terri & Gerry Baugus
Lissi Bedford
Bharat B. Behan
Bob & Judy Bell
The Robert Belstock Family
Laura Phillips Bence
Ed & Anie Bergo
Bob & Paula Berka
Marjorie S. Beyer
George & Winnie Biocini
Ann & Pete Bjorklund
Dorothy & Emma Blake
Eric Hamilton Blanding
Mardell & Gerry Blaufarb
The Blomstrom Family
Judy & Dick Bogard
Mary Ann & John Bogart
Ellen & Chris Bowen
Roger & Penny Brunello
Dan & Linda Brunello
Scott & Natalie Brunello
Ada Brunello
Mike & Marge Bruno
L.G. "Boo" Bue
The Frederick L. Butterworth Family
California Water Service
Bob & Barbara Callison
Judy Hoffmann, Campi Properties
Will & Sharron Carleton
Bill & Virginia Carlsen
Lucy Ann Carlton, Chief of Police
Arthur & Jean Carmichael
Arthur Carmichael
Jennifer Carmichael
Kris & Harold Casto
Pat & Tami Cavaney
Lisa Chanoff
Chloe
Annalisa Choy
Dorothy & Pete Christiansen
Walter & Vera Chronert
Citibank-Foothill Plaza
Citibank-Main Street
City of Los Altos
Dean & Linda Clark
Jo & Kim Clark
Bob & Carol Clarke
Pam & Christy Clarke
Eric, Lee & Christian Clemmensen
Coldwell Banker
Ernest & Virginia Conrad
The Lloyd Corliss Family

Jim & Emily Courtice
The Courture Family
Sue & Clyde Cummings
The Cummins Family
Custom Artistry by Denise
Carol Curran D'Augusta
Bob & Judy Dahl
George & Luna Dai
Elayne & Phil Dauber
Joe & Gayle Davis
Herb & Bette Davis
Glenn & Pauline DeKraker
The Delta Group
Waltraud Dewers
Wayne B. & Sabra R. Dexter
Bill & Ginny Dolan
Eula Dolby
Patricia Dowd, LAH City Clerk
Augustin & Christiane Dubrulle
Jane Duffy
Steve & Diane Dunham
The Roy Dunnett Family
Arthur W. Dusenberry
William & Hilda Eaton
Paul Eckert, Eckert & Co. Prop.
Marilyn J. Edwardson
Natalie & Ralph Elefant
The Dave Ellsworth Family
Sylvia & Roger Eng
The Michael T. English Family
George Estill & Family
EurekaBank
Excel Pool & Patio, Inc.
Expressions, Inc.
Phil & Sheila Faillace & Daughters
Florence Fava McCliman
Rick Feldner, Realtor
Jarin & Carole Feldstein
Jan & Bob Fenwick
Cathy & Bruce Fielding
Audrey Fisher
Anna Knapp Fitz
Ray Flanegan, Coldwell Banker
Wayne & Donna Fleming
Bob & Joan Foerster
Colvin J. & Katherine Fontenot
Foothills Congregational Church UCC
Dick & Nancy Fouquet
Paul & Dona Frakes
Chet & Pat Frankenfield
Roger & Mabel Frelier
Mary & Douglas Fries
Brian A. Funk & Friends
The George Furuichi Family
Al & Carol Galedrige
Hank & Phyllis Gauthier
Charlene & Jim Geers
Dianne Gershuny
Nan & Chuck Geschke
Omar & Vallee Ghoseh
Mim Gibbs
Ellen Akerlund Gonella
Paul J. Gonella
Joe & Hon Mai Goodman
Peggy Gordon
Edward S. Gorzynski, Jr. & Family
Bob & Peggy Grady
Graphicstat, Inc.

Marion & Bob Grimm
Thomas & Carolyn Grimm
Michael Grimm
Patty Grimm
Don & Lana Grant
Dave & Dee Gustavson
Vernon & Martha Gustavson
Jeff & Katie Haisley
Dan & Olivia Haley
Thelma & George Halverson
Tim & Cammie Hanley
Pat Hanlock
Judy & Bill Hannemann
James B. Harris
Dick & Mary Hasenpflug
Ernest L. Hawks
Loraine F. Hawks
Eric K. Hawks
Jennifer A. Hawks
Harriet & Dave Heebink
Lee & Sue Heesacker
Jack & Janice Heidmiller
Susan Heintzelman
Conrad Heintzelman
Dick, Paulette & Tom Henning
Ed & Arie Hodges
Judy & Dave Hoffmann
Elise & Terry Holst
Sid & Doni Hubbard
Audry Hubbard
Jack & Bobbie Huston
The Initial Stitch
Ingrid Jackson
Yvonne Jacobson
Sylvia & Ben Johnson & Family
Heidi & Whitney Johnson
Mary Jane Johnston
Neil & Stephanie Johnston
Crayton & Sandy Jones
Bob & Betty Joss
Jennifer E. Joss
Randall M. Joss
Elizabeth Joss & Associates
Murphy Joss CD
Shizu Jumura
Mel & Mady Kahn
Kahn's Corner Pharmacy
Martha E. Kambe, CPA
Ginne & Bill Kaufmann
Toshiko Furuichi Kawamoto
Les & Mary Kaye
Kenneth R. Kaye, Atty at Law
Bill & Marjorie Kellogg
Lucille Kendall
Kentucky Fried Chicken
Ted & Judi Keyani
Robert Kleiner
Rose Kleiner
Allison Phillips Klotz
Keith & Ruth Koehler
Fred Beronio, Evelyn Beronio Koenig
Bill & Terry Krivan
Ben & Helen Kuckens
Laszlo & Gabriella Kurczinak
David E. Lambourne, State Farm Ins.
Richard & Gabrielle Landrum
Peter & Caroline Landsbergen
Douglas & Linda Lanterman

Roy Lave
Penny Lave
Julia Lave
Reynolds Lave
Lawson-Hawks Ins. Agency
Joe & Sandy Leal
Ginny & King Lear
LeBoulanger
Robert & Denise Lerch
Stephanie Lester
Noreen & Dick Letts
Fred & Harriet Levien
The Richard Liewer Family
Ann & George Limbach
Sandra & Douglas Limbach
Jean & Alan Limbach
David Limbach
Natalie Limbach
Linden Tree, Children's Records/Books
Los Altos Board of Realtors
Los Altos Chamber of Commerce
Los Altos Conservatory Theatre
Los Altos Garbage Company
Los Altos Library
Los Altos Pharmacy
Los Altos Rotary Club
Los Altos School District
The Los Atos Village Association
Loyola Corners Business Assn
Cynthia M. Luedtke
David L. Luedtke
Matthew D. Luedtke
Bob & Ruth Lundquist
Peggy & John Lynch
Lee Lynch
The Frank Mack Family
The Mackenzie Group
Larry, Dena, Cindy, Dona & Sue Madsen
Main Street Antiques
Maria's Antiques of Los Altos
Dona & Pat Marriott
Wendy & Julian Marshall
Alan & Nancy Marston
Gary & Vicki Martin
Bobbie & Charlie Maschal
Nancy & Larry Mason
The Leonard McBirney Family
Tom & Barbara McCarthy
Edgar A. McDowell
Rory & Lindy McGowan
Joan & Jack McMenomey
Karen Melbye
Mr. & Mrs. L.J. Mikula
Pauline & Eric Millar
The Bill Mingus Family
Becky & Jim Morgan
Michael & Suzanne Moshier
Dr. and Mrs. Doyne Mraz
Douglas Munson
Ron & Anne Murphy
Alexander & Suzanne Myers
Robert & Irene Myrback
Clinton & Susan Nagy
Jennifer Shaw Navarrete
Scott Neely
In memory of Larry & Bea Nelson
Tom & Barbara Nelson
Todd & Tiffany Nelson
Ann & Warren Nelson
Kent & Cary Nelson
The Bart Nelson Family
Jean Newton
Paul & Ellen Noble
Alice & Rick Nuzzo
Liz & Paul Nyberg
Dan & Suzanne Nyberg
Dave & Rhonda Nyberg
Jonathan Paul Nyberg
Bud & Ann Oliver
Carl & Myra Orta
Don & Dianne Overbo
Stephen D. & Louise A. Pahl
Jayne H. Parker
JoAnne & Jack Parks
Don & Norma Patterson
Ann & George Perham
Dr. & Mrs. Samuel Pesner
Jill & Steve Peterson
Howard & Barbara Phillips
Jon & Barbara Phillips
Louis & AnnaMae Piro
The Polata Family
Sally & Russ Porter
Postal Express
Ruth Powell
The Joe Presti Family
Print Innovations, Inc.
Mary Prochnow
Rancho Travel
Raj & Anita Reddy
The Jane & John Reed Family
Dave & Vicki Reeder
Julie & Jason Reeder
Reitmeir's Werkstatt, Inc.
Jim Reynolds
Jane R. Ridgway
Bill & Lorraine Rieder
Lonny J. Rittler
Virginia Roberts
Bob & Mary Rogers
James R. Rogers
Julie & Mike Rose
Matthew J. Rossow Agricultural Services
Vernon & Ruth Rossow
The Earle Rother, Sr. Family
Mel, Vicci & Doron Rudin
Billy B. & Tish Russell
Margaret Salameda
Denis & Kristine Salmon
Erin Salmon
Brenden Salmon
Kari Salmon
Charles B. Sandoval
Santa Clara Library
Christiana Schaefer
Drew Schaefer
Carol Scharz
Charles & Cristine Schill
Chad, Linda, Stacey & Cas Schneller
Kathleen & Wulf Schrader
Harry & Ingrid Schrader
Seville Properties
Dale & Margo Seymour
Bob & Sue Shaffer
Mrs. Ellen Shaw
Rosemary Shaw
Shelton Roofing Co. Inc.
Damon & Judy Simpson
Marie A. Singer
Katrina Smathers
K. Rey & Susan Smith
Mike & Ann Smith
The Carl Snyder Family
Bill & Elaine Spaller
Louise & Denny Spangler
Anne Spangler
Amy Spangler
Sarah Spangler
Honor Spitz
Brian Spitz
Eric Spitz
Mason & Sue St. John-Gilbert
Wm. Clinton & Judith A. Steele
Goodwin & Gerry Steinberg
Helen Stevens
Cynthia Louise Strand
Amy Elizabeth Strand
Albert & Marilyn Stratz
Vi Sullivan
Beatrice Surbridge
Linda G. & John E. Swan
Alan Swanson, CPA
Mr & Mrs Joseph J. Sweeney
Tig & Marilyn Tarlton
Brown, Rosalie, Alison Taylor
Beatrice J. Teer
Carol & Gaylord Tefft Family
Jean C. Thacher
Mrs. E.N.C. (Margaret) Thompson
Lewis & Ann Throop
Diane & Roger Tonnesen
The Tossy Family
The J. Trant Family
Fritz & Nomi Trapnell
The Tom Tripiano Family
The J. Truant Family
Sally & Ed Truitt
Diane Tupper
Edwin J. Turney
Uncommon Threads
Nick Vaksuik
Michelle Valine
Gene & Mary van Tamelen
George J. & Betty Jo Vlay
Peter J. Volarvich Family
Dr. & Mrs. S. Wallace
Dr. Masao & Eleanor Watanabe
Josh & Laurel Watanabe
Dr. Chris & Georgia Watson & Family
William & Bethel Watt
Sisi Weaver
Fran & Don Weiler
Betsy Spangler Westman
Pinky & Chuck Whelan
Bill Wilson
Ed & Charlotte Winguth
Fred & Lois Wolcott
Peter & Marguerite Wolford
Woodland Library
The Yort Family
Dennis & Roberta Young
David R. Young
Young, Craig & Co. CPAs
Christopher Munro Young
David R. Young
Bob & Edna Yoxall
Cameron Zschau
Ed & Jo Zschau
Ed Zschau, Jr.
Elizabeth Zschau

Historical Timeline

Events that have shaped the community.

1542 Cabrillo discovers California.
1769 Don Gaspar de Portola visits area in search of Monterey Bay.
1776 Juan Bautista de Anza party travels from Mexico to San Francisco.
1833 Mexican Secularization Act strips Franciscans of California land holdings.
1839 Rancho San Antonio granted to Don Juan Prado.
1840 Rancho Purissima Concepcion, 5000 acres, granted to Indians, Jose Gregorio and Jose Ramon.
1845 Don Juan Prado builds adobe house on El Monte Road.
1847 Rancho Purissima Concepcion purchased by Juana Briones de Miranda.
1850 Adobe house built on Old Trace Road in Los Altos Hills by Juana Briones.
1852 Ohlone Indian Bay Area population estimated at 110,000; 15,000 by 1900.
1861 John Snyder purchases 650 acre ranch, begins farming, new to area.
1888 Sarah Winchester purchases ranches on site of what later became Los Altos.
1901 J. Gilbert Smith buys five acres, plants apricot orchard. now Civic Center.
1901 Purissima School built, now Chapel in the Hills.
1903 Harry Lee Brubaker builds home on farm on Purissima Road, now Los Altos Hills.
1904 University of Santa Clara purchases 700 acres to build school near Loyola Corners.
1905 Edwin L. Emerson family moves into new home at Miramonte and Covington.
1906 Southern Pacific Railroad purchases 100 acres from Sarah Winchester.
1906 University of Santa Clara abandons plans to build school in Los Altos.
1906 Town site named Banks and Braes by SP, changed to Los Altos by1907
1907 Town site laid out by Altos Land Company.
1907 First SP railway station opens in two box cars.
1908 Approximate date when Chandler School for Girls opens in former Merriman House on Edgewood Lane.
1908 First elementary school classes meet in Shoup Hall.
1908 First commercial business opens: Eschenbruecher Hardware store and post office.
1908 Los Altos Star newspaper published by Walter A. Clark, printed only a few issues.
1908 Telephone service installed.
1910 Little Gables home built by Morgans prior to Morgan Manor development.
1910 Powerhouse for electric railway built.
1911 Twelve trains a day pass through Los Altos.
1911 Los Altos Grammar School built at San Antonio Road and Hillview Avenue.
1911 Water Works opens, $1 per house per month.
1912 Ramsey's garage at First and State Streets is built.
1913 New railroad depot completed by Southern Pacific.
1913 Union Church organized and opens Easter Sunday with 20 charter members.
1914 Episcopal Church builds church on Orange Avenue.
1914 Construction of Morgan Manor begins, later becomes Ford Country Day School.
1914 Union Church builds "little brown church"on San Antonio Road.
1914 First library opens with100 books in Altos Land Company office at First and Main.
1915 Toyon Dairy Farm established with 30 to 40 head of cattle.
1915 Los Altos Improvement Club formed campaigning for better roads to the city.
1915 Los Altos Star newspaper restarted by H. G. Copeland.
1916 Voters registered: 216 Republicans; 123 Democrats; 23 Socialists; 9 Prohibitionists.
1917 Rand McNally Road Atlas lists Los Altos population at 60.
1918 Ng Tong Temple, open-air pavilion for plays, opens in what will later become Shoup Park.
1919 First National Bank opens at First and Main: $25,000 capital and $5,000 surplus.
1922 Tom Woodworth organizes first fire fighting unit.
1922 Two wings added to San Antonio School.
1922 Scout Hall on First Street completed; later used as library.
1923 620 acres purchased by Los Altos Golf and Country Club from Santa Clara University.
1923 St. Joseph College purchases Snyder Ranch.
1924 Duvenecks purchase Hidden Villa.
1924 Los Altos Water Company has 230 paying patrons.

1925 El Retiro opens as a retreat house on former Wellman estate.
1925 F. L. Rathbun opens first plumbing shop near First and Main Streets.
1926 St. Joseph's College Seminary opens for students preparing for priesthood.
1929 New fire truck purchased: 1929 Ford, Model A one ton truck, still on display at fire house.
1931 First Volunteer Fire Department organized at Ramsey's Garage.
1932 William Formway Machine Shop on Almond Avenue begins manufacturing Wizard Walnut Huller.
1933 Peninsular Electric Railroad ceases operations due to lack of customers.
1935 Library moves to deserted powerhouse on First Street.
1937 Hidden Villa Youth Hostel opens, first in the West.
1938 Los Altos assigned WHitecliff telephone prefix, i. e. WH 8-5555.
1939 Los Altos Fire District formed.
1939 Kahn Pharmacy took over the Gregery and Shoup Pharmacy at First and Main Streets.
1939 John & Sal's Italian Grocery opens on San Antonio near Pine Lane, now Mark Twain apartments.
1942 Artillery shell from Army training camp at Page Mill explodes in attic of residence on Second Street.
1947 Kiwanis Club organized.
1947 First issue of Town Crier published in September.
1949 Movie theater opens on Main Street, 74 cents for adults.
1949 Los Altos Rotary Club founded by Guy Shoup.
1950 First National Bank opens in new building at Third and Main Streets.
1950 Los Altos Morning Forum holds first meeting.
1950 Chamber of Commerce organized by Business Men's Association.
1951 Rancho Shopping Center opens with 30 shops.
1952 Black Forest Inn opens, changed to Silan Restaurant in 1999.
1952 Los Altos incorporated as city, December 1.
1953 Los Altos/Mountain View chapter of American Association of University Women chartered.
1953 Police Department established by City Council.
1953 Ligtelyn Travel Counselors opens for business on Main Street.
1955 Ford Country Day School opens at Morgan Manor, reverting to private residence in 1986.
1956 Friends of the Library founded by AAUW.
1956 Los Altos Hills incorporated as a town.
1957 Library Commission established.
1958 Downtown Parking Plaza completed providing 1000 free parking places.
1958 City owned sewage treatment plant operational near the San Francisco Bay on San Antonio Road.
1958 Southern Pacific discontinues passenger service to Los Altos.
1959 Los Altos Rotary Club formed.
1959 City Hall completed at 1 North San Antonio Road.
1959 Bing Crosby pledges $10,000 for new Youth Center.
1959 The League of Women Voters of Los Altos, Los Altos Hills, and Mountain View established.
1960 Youth Center completed in Civic Center.
1961 Census shows population of Los Altos: 19,696; Los Altos Hills: 3412
1961 Foothill College moves to new campus.
1961 El Camino Hospital opens to serve the Los Altos area.
1961 Chamber of Commerce moves to present building at University and Burke Avenues.
1964 Sheldon of Los Altos opens for business at 380 Main Street.
1964 New library building in civic center dedicated.
1964 Downtown Village Association formed.
1964 Last train (freight) passed through Los Altos.
1965 Foothill Expressway opens, replacing railroad tracks.
1965 Shoup Park dedicated after extensive renovation.
1967 Shoreline Alternative High School formed.
1971 Ohlone village site unearthed near El Monte and O'Keefe Lane.
1973 City buys Hillview School and creates the Hillview Community Center.
1974 Heritage Oaks Park purchased by City at Portland and Miramonte Avenues.

1974 Redwood Grove Nature Preserve acquired by the city.
1974 Los Altos Grammar School at Hillview and San Antonio razed for commercial office buildings.
1974 Historical Commission established to open J. Gilbert Smith House as a City Museum.
1976 Reenactment of Anza party trek on its 200th anniversary
1976 Fountain designed by Larry Madsen installed at the main library.
1977 History House opens December 1 on City of Los Altos 25th anniversary of incorporation.
1978 Westwind Barn handicapped program begins.
1978 Adobe Creek Lodge on Moody Road closes.
1979 City buys land from Medical Mission Sisters for park on Fremont Avenue near Grant Road.
1985 Eschenbruecher home, on Second street moved to Los Altos Hills as Heritage House.
1986 Ford Country Day School (Morgan Manor) reverts to private residence.
1987 Sister Cities organization formed.
1988 Los Altos City Hall expansion completed.
1988 Town Crier sold by Terrance Donnally to Chicago Tribune.
1989 Last major Los Altos orchard converted to home sites at Grant Road.
1989 Lincoln Park gazebo completed.
1989 Alpha Omega program to aid homeless launched by churches and CSA.
1989 Neary Quarry in Los Altos Hills closed, land converted to homesites.
1989 Farmers' Market at Loyola Corners begins, moves to Foothill College in 1999
1992 Los Altos Tomorrow launched with $41,000 contributed by 16 founders.
1992 Los Altos Library expansion completed.
1992 El Camino Hospital District transferred to a non-profit organization.
1993 Town Crier purchased from Chicago Tribune on March 15 by local owners.
1993 Community Plaza completed at Main and State streets in downtown Los Altos.
1994 Bus Barn Stage Company formed after demise of L'ACT.
1995 Rep. Tom Campbell speaks to first Los Altos Community Prayer Breakfast.
1995 Los Altos Online web site launched for community by Town Crier.
1995 Shoreline High School changes name to Alta Vista High School.
1995 Chef Lawrence Chu chosen as first Los Altan of the Year by the Town Crier.
1996 El Camino Hospital District Board regains control of hospital.
1996 Los Altos Tomorrow changes name to Los Altos Community Foundation.
1996 Palm Pilot developed by Los Altos based startup.
1996 LAH resident, David Packard dies, foundation assets reach $10 billion by 1999.
1996 City purchases lots at First and Main Streets for parking development.
1997 $300,000 science and technology fund drive completed for library.
1997 After 50 years in business, McElroy Lumber building razed, replaced by Gateway Building.
1997 St. Williams school site at Rosita Drive is purchased by city for public park.
1997 Los Altos History House Museum celebrates its 20th anniversary.
1997 Foothill Bank becomes Bank of Los Altos.
1997 Day worker center opens on El Camino.
1998 Los Altos Community Foundation acquires a "home" at 183 Hillview Avenue.
1998 Los Altos History House Museum Association celebrates its 20th anniversary.
1998 Al's Barber Shop has operated continuously for 50 years.
1998 Festival of Lights celebrates its 25th anniversary.
1998 Veterans' Memorial dedicated July 4 in Shoup Park.
1998 Los Altos/Mountain View high schools remodeling begins.
1998 $94 million bond for elementary school remodeling passes with 75% margin.
1999 Construction of the Education Center at History House begins.
1999 Park at Edith and San Antonio completed, named Conner Park.
1999 Youth Commission formed by Los Altos City Council.
1999 Rosita Park dedicated

INDEX

INDEX